The Worst Journey
in the Midlands

D1327098

Sam Llewellyn

The Worst Journey in the Midlands

with line drawings by Chris Aggs

'Of rowing, as of other carnal pleasures,
cometh satiety at the last.'
Charles Kingsley, *Hypatia*

HEINEMANN : LONDON

William Heinemann Ltd
10 Upper Grosvenor Street, London W1X 9PA
LONDON   MELBOURNE   TORONTO
JOHANNESBURG   AUCKLAND

First published 1983

SBN 434 42745 4

Map by Paul Davies

Photoset by Parker Typesetting Service, Leicester
Printed in Great Britain by
St Edmundsbury Press, Bury St Edmunds, Suffolk

To Karen, Willie and Martin

Acknowledgements

There are many people without whose help the Worst Journey in the Midlands could never had been made. I would like to thank them all, particularly Will of the Maesllwch Arms Hotel, Glasbury, Britain's premier Canadian canoeist, who lent me one of his hire craft for the first phase of the journey, and subsequently extended the hospitality of the Maesllwch's unrivalled cellar and kitchens.

I must also acknowledge my deep debts to Bun and Nigel Thimbleby, Sarah and David Burnett, Martin Adams, Stella and Martin Wilkinson, Linda Hill, Belinda and Tim Hextall, Briony and Andrew Lawson, Jenny and Tony Ellerton, and Nic Barlow.

My survival is entirely due to all those who offered a timely tow rope; my thanks to all of them, particularly Bingo and Dilys Smail in *Dyfed*, who saved my life and no error.

Contents

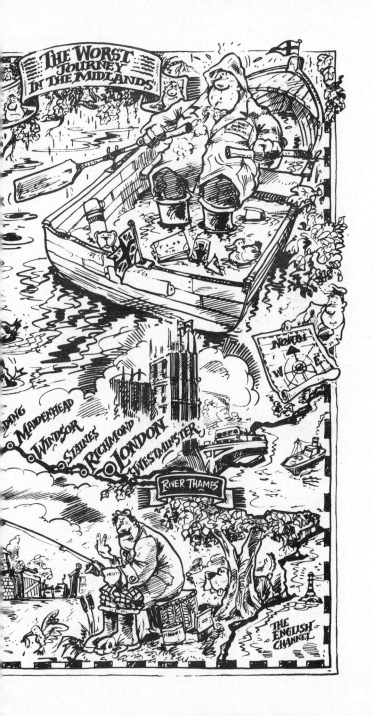

PROLOGUE

High on the eastern slopes of Plynlimmon, there is a tiny pool floored with grey stones. The water is clear, but filled with little currents, perpetually bubbling from the springs below. The overflow rushes enthusiastically down the side of the mountain's vast green dome, joining others like itself, hurling itself over precipices and barging through thickets of scrub and bramble. As it swells, the shoulders of the hills rise on either side; soon it is racing down towards the roofs of Llanidloes, a market town straddling the throat of the valley. Under the town bridge the river runs ten yards wide, crystal clear between beaches of grey pebbles. It has become the Severn.

On a drizzly morning in early October, I was standing under the bridge holding an aluminium canoe, thinking solemn thoughts before setting out on the first stage of a long journey. The early part of the journey was down the young Severn to Welshpool, a good stretch for fishing but a bad one for boating.

As far as Welshpool I would travel in this canoe, which was tough enough to navigate water where most boats would end up as firewood. At Welshpool, I was to transfer to my antique rowing boat *Magdalen*, and proceed in dignified luxury down the now less rocky Severn to Tewkesbury, up the Avon to Warwick, along the Grand Union to Napton, down the Oxford Canal to Oxford, and down the Thames to London. Three hundred and fifty miles in all. A long way to go backwards.

As I dropped the canoe in the water and pushed off, I wondered why – apart from the fact that it had never been done before – I was doing this thing.

The houses of Llanidloes fell away; the trees came up to meet me, and under them the roar of the first rapids.

I planned to find out on the way.

Part One

CHAPTER ONE

Preparation

*A walk on the beach – Narrative of the Bure disaster – Birth of an idea –
A boat is found – Special features of* Magdalen *– Magdalen under the
knife – Clinker building – Boat-building for taxidermists – The Anvil
Chorus – Incredulity in a gravel pit – Portable gastronomy – Equipment
and omens – Probable attitude of posterity – Probable outcome of
expedition*

Early in September 1982, I was walking on the shingle at Ringstead Bay in Dorset. A warm breeze was blowing; the sun rode high to the south-west, frosting the blue ripples towards Portland Bill. With me was Smokey Joe Cordwainer, craftsman kipper-manufacturer and general-purpose sage.

Smokey lives above the beach. He had been keeping his eye on the rowing boat *Magdalen*, whose owner, George Glover, had several years previously parked her in the Ringstead dunes and gone about his business. Smokey reckoned that she would be rotten as cheese, by now. As we walked, we spoke of the unknown corners of the world, and the desirability or otherwise of ripping the veils from them. At least I did; Smokey was wagging his head in silence.

'Daft bugger,' he said finally. Since there was nobody else on the beach, I had to assume he was talking to me. The Smoke has a firm grip on the practicalities of life, and if he says you are a daft bugger you can be sure that a large segment of the population shares his view.

We crunched on. At last he turned his massive shoulders towards the dunes and said, 'She's in there.' We walked up a narrow path in the marram grass. The buzzing of flies became audible over the rustle of the breeze. Cheery festoons of Andrex bore witness to Ringstead Bay's popularity with the all-night angling fraternity. Under a bramble bush, there was a flash of sun-bleached mahogany and flaking paint. I found my breathing quickening and wished it wouldn't, because the smell was horrible.

'Nobody's touched her for years,' said Smokey. 'Except to use her as a lavatory. You're out of your tiny mind.'

And of course he was quite right.

There are, however, influences that make more pressing demands on the human soul than mere logic. It happened that this afternoon such influences were operating on me; I needed a boat, and I needed one fast and cheap. And there it was, under that bramble bush, and its name was *Magdalen*.

The story began when I was thirteen years old, and set off with a group of other boys to travel in kayaks down the River Bure, ending in the Norfolk Broads. It was the sort of expedition that the Famous Five would have undertaken with one hand tied behind its back. We were going to camp, and so on.

Kayaks are heavy. You have to carry them round barbed-wire fences, full of tents and tin cans. I must have been rather a weak youth because I remember panting a lot and wishing I had never started. My main contribution to the expedition was a new kind of methylated spirit stove. In recognition of the stove, my companions chose to overlook my feebleness at the paddle and portage, waiting for this wonder to reveal itself. When we arrived at the camping place, I lit it. Small blue flames wobbled disappointingly. Hoping to ginger it up, I applied more methylated spirits. There was an explosion. When I returned to myself, the tent roof was burning briskly.

Telephone calls were made. The tent was mended, with parental assistance. Night began to fall. We gathered round the camp-fire (the stove had been declared a write-off). 'Well,' I said. 'On we go, eh?'

Five pairs of eyes homed in. 'No,' said the leader, a cold-eyed Aryan who now works for the *Financial Times*. 'We've had a talk. We're packing it in.'

'Before supper?'

'It's all yours,' he said, and vanished into the night.

I still bear the mental scars. They cause me to sweat freely and groan aloud on crowded tube-trains. It was after one such groaning session, conducted in private with an atlas on the knee, that my eye lit on a map of Wales.

On the eastern slopes of Plynlimmon, it was caught by a whiskery blue line. This was the tail of the infant Severn. The eye travelled eastward, down rapids and along stately glides, through gorges filled with the thunder of mighty waters and into quieter reaches where half-timbered houses jutted over swans admiring their reflections, and grizzled lock-keepers sipped pints of nut-brown ale beside canals noisy with the brilliant paintwork and terrible oaths of the narrow-boat folk. And on either side of the blue line cities closed in, Worcester and Birmingham, Warwick and Leamington Spa, their vast chimneys clouding the Heart of England; and then came the Oxford Canal, where mayhap a don would be mumbling Greek to a smock-frocked scholar-shepherd; and below Oxford itself Old Father Thames, rolling, just keeping on rolling through its panoply of bridges to the grey sea and the Mother of Parliaments.

The eye ceased to track, clouded with tears of destiny fulfilled. All I needed was a boat.

I live near Ludlow in Shropshire, which is nearly as far from the sea as Milton Keynes. Ludlow is not an ideal spot for finding boats. There is supposed to have been one there once but nobody was interested in it and it went away. The nearby Welsh borders are full of canoes, of course, but canoes are not what they were in the days of Hiawatha. The dominant species of canoe is the kayak and kayaks are filled with horrid memories for me, even subsequent to the Bure disaster. Broad-hipped people such as myself have difficulty in getting into them and worse difficulty getting out. Once, in Ireland, someone forced me into one, gave me a life-jacket and pointed me at a vast Guinness-coloured weir on the River Blackwater. Talented performers can right their kayaks with the Eskimo roll. I was not talented enough for that. A rock popped up and knocked me over. I went down the weir on my side, unable to wriggle out of the plastic cigar trapping those portions of me below the waist, but kept afloat by the life-jacket. Apparently I was screaming thinly.

Canadian canoes are more fun and certainly more acceptable aesthetically; but they are too easy. A coracle was too small, too slow, too unpredictable and too Celtic. It looked as if it would have to be a rowing boat. There was apparently only one rowing boat available in the country; a cockleshell jewel less than ten feet long, built from solid mahogany for Queen Victoria's navy. A boat of mellowness and charm. *Magdalen*.

A boat rotten to the core, full of holes, lying under a bramble bush in an al fresco carsey in the dunes behind Ringstead Bay. *Magdalen*.

So there you are. Up to date.

A week after my stroll with Smokey I borrowed a Land-Rover and trailer and went to pick the boat up. As I roared through the late-summer lanes of North Dorset, I was aware of a certain unease. Possibly I had not looked at *Magdalen* hard enough. I had used her five years earlier, to haul a trammel net set for red mullet in Ringstead Bay. Dim memories of copious leakage kept returning. She didn't look as if she had been moved since we left her, up there in the dunes. Five years was a longish time. Possibly I should have spiked her with a bradawl, or anyway pulled the bramble bush off her, before committing myself.

Come now, I said, wrenching the Land-Rover out of the path of an oncoming combine harvester, you haven't *really* committed yourself. You are free at any moment to abandon the whole enterprise. The fact that you have by now told about five hundred people about your plan is irrelevant. They will merely think you are all talk and no action. Situation normal.

Engaging four-wheel drive, I began climbing out of the ditch. The transmission howled in my ears, but the derisive voices howled louder. I was back round the camp-fire again, under the chilly scrutiny of the Kayak Gauleiter. And I knew that no matter how rotten *Magdalen* might be, I would have to fix her up somehow.

There was no backing out now.

Soon afterwards I picked up George Glover, *Magdalen*'s owner, from the fortified manor house in which he lives. George is pretty keen on old things, and is a connoisseur of the derelict. Even, so, when he saw the boat he fell silent. This affected me curiously, arousing perverse instincts of protection. I tore aside the brambles, exposing *Magdalen*'s peeling belly, then gripped her gunwale and turned her over. Throwing away the chunks of gunwale that remained in my hand, I dragged her down to the water, which was clear and blue and bubbled enthusiastically through the perforations in her bottom. Climbing in, I rowed her towards the slipway. She took ten minutes to fill completely, and did not capsize until she was nearly there. This was encouraging.

George kept silent as we dragged her up the beach. When she was on the trailer he said, in his ruminative way: 'I don't think I've ever seen a boat bend quite like that.'

'Amazing,' I agreed. 'Wonderful bit of construction.'

'Hmm.' He leaned his knee against the side. It bulged inwards as if made of paper. 'She's always been a bit . . . weak that side.'

'Soon fix her up,' I said, with maniac zest.

'Hmm,' said George, and we went back to his house for lunch.

Emmett Manor, George's house, was a powerful incitement to mellowness. Bees droned over the flagstones of the courtyard, Red Admirals posed on late lilacs, and the last swallows threaded the battlements. I set out for home under a brilliant blue sky with *Magdalen* on the trailer and a feeling that everything was for the best in the best of all possible worlds.

By degrees, the spell faded. *Magdalen* bounced in the rear-view mirror, piebald with peeling paint. I had seen quite a lot of rotten boats, and there was no denying that *Magdalen* was one of the rottenest. She was, in fact, a derelict. Yet I had promised myself that I would be on the water in a month. By the time I got home, I was convinced that the whole venture, and particularly *Magdalen*, was doomed. I dragged her into the workshop, locked the doors, and, according to my policy in these circumstances, hoped she would go away.

It worked well enough for a couple of days. But then Karen, my wife, pulled up all the carrots in the garden, laid them out on the workshop floor, and began to ask in a pointed manner where she was going to put the beetroot – in or out of the boat, since it looked as if it would be there all winter. And the boys, Willie, four, and Martin, two, took to going on long ocean voyages in her, and leaping about repelling boarders and discovering *terrae incognitae* while lumps of rotten mahogany crumbled under their little gumboots. People kept asking when I was setting off, so I manufactured a date; the third of October, I said; beginning of season of mists and mellow fruitfulness, characterized, meteorologists tell us, by north-westerly gales and solid, river-swelling rainfall, both of which would speed my progress towards London. Really, how fascinating, they said, their eyes glazing with mingled boredom and disbelief.

September trickled away. Every day the boys brought in new bits of debris from the shed, and every night I dreamed of *Magdalen*, derelict.

On 14 September, I caved in, and started trying to do something to make her float.

Magdalen was clinker built of once-solid mahogany, and had originally been painted white on the outside and varnished on the inside. There were two sets of holes into which rowlocks were designed to be fitted with a bow thwart convenient for one set and a middle thwart convenient for the other. The after thwart was convenient for nothing at all, being impossible to sit on by reason of the huge ring-bolt that protruded from the centre of the transom. Once upon a time she had been very attractive. Not any more. On her outside, she looked as if she had leprosy; on her inside, gangrene.

The skeleton of a clinker-built boat is stem, keel, transom and ribs. To the ribs planks are riveted in such a way that they overlap; these planks are then sewn along their edges with copper rivets. It is a method of construction that is becoming obsolete because of its expense – each plank must be individually cut to shape – and because new materials like fibreglass are stronger and require less maintenance.

A sound clinker-built boat has a beauty all of its own: a lovely flare of the bow, a delicately wineglass-shaped transom, and a pleasing enhancement of the bulbousness of the gunwales by the lines of the planks' edges. In addition, the double reinforcement of overlapped planks riveted to ribs gives it the resilience of a basket or a cricket ball.

An unsound clinker-built boat is one of the most monstrous aberrations known to man. If the wood is not scraped and painted annually, it soaks up water and rots. The favourite place for rotting is under the ribs, where sand, gravel, seaweed, dead fish and Mars bar wrappers make little dams behind which pools of water form. In time, the ribs come to resemble Edinburgh rock, and the planks next to them soften and crumble. This process is accelerated by stress factors such as shipwreck.

At some time in the 1920s, *Magdalen* must have been in collision with a boulder. The shattered planks on her starboard side had been patched with copper sheeting, nailed over a mess of tar and old string. This was now flaking away like the skin of a diseased onion. Once it had been stripped off, the naked timbers, viewed from below, had a gauzy transparency not unlike Brussels lace.

In order to test a wooden boat's soundness, you stab it with a bradawl. Distributing bradawl and courage between both hands, I marched solemnly round *Magdalen*, prodding. Forty stabs later, she looked like a colander. It was possible to read a paperback under her upturned hull without artificial light.

There is no good way of repairing a rotten and smashed plank except to take it out and put in a new one. With clinker-built boats this is problematical; due to the radical curves inflicted by the boat-builder on his strips of wood, they tend to adopt a one-out, all-out policy known as springing. A clinker-built boat springing is a process which veterans compare with a Kansas twister in a woodshed. What happens is that as soon as the vital rivet is removed, the boat (usually inverted) begins to writhe like a living thing. This is the signal for the artificer to withdraw, for within seconds the writhing becomes a bronco-like bucking, with smashed rivets whizzing about like rifle bullets. Shortly afterwards, plank separates from plank, humming across the workshop like a demented mowing machine and felling all in its path. At last, all is silence and a pile of kindling; of the boat no trace remains.

Since the invention of fibreglass, the boat-builder's life might be thought to have become easier. Unfortunately, not so. This is because wood, when moistened, swells, while plastic does not. Early boat-builders' attempts at patching with fibreglass terminated in terrible rending noises and gouts of green sea-water as the timbers literally tore themselves apart. The parable of the new wine in old bottles should have been lesson enough – indeed, many paid heed. Unfortunately, however, the New Testament is a bit reticent about alternatives to fibreglass.

For the record, alternatives considered for *Magdalen* were: more copper sheeting, home insulation foam, clay, tar, canvas, wine-bottle corks, and a good thick coat of paint (this last rejected because there is no paint currently on the market capable of spanning a two-inch hole). Eventually, I rang up a boat-yard in Shrewsbury where a cheery voice said, 'Silicone sealant.'

When I arrived at the yard, there was nobody there. Calling forlornly, I wandered into an upper room. There was a strange and terrible smell; rotting flesh combined with pungent chemicals. A thin man looked up from a table at the far end. I told him what I wanted, and he began unloading tubes of the stuff from a crate. There were no boats in evidence. I asked him what he was using it for.

'Stuffing,' he said.

'What?'

'Stuffing.' He held up the thing he had been working on. It was a dead stoat. Into a certain part of its anatomy was thrust the nozzle of a grease gun. Gripped in the gun was a tube of silicone sealant.

I gathered up my tubes, made my excuses and left.

The tempo of repair work quickened once I discovered you could fill quite big holes with flexible plastic padding. Waxing ambitious, I decided to make new ribs to replace the old ones, which were rotten. I got a lot of ash strips and boiled them in a dustbin until they bent. Then I nailed them in. It looked quite professional.

After the ribs came the planking. There were large areas where the prodding finger left deep indentations, or, in extreme cases, went right through. I therefore set to work to scrape away all the rot and corruption, and in the process managed to run a half-inch blade of putrescent mahogany up behind the nail of my right forefinger. It was at that point that I decided all I was going to do about the rot was to paint over it except where the daylight showed through, in which case plastic padding would be called into play. This bold decision speeded things up a good deal, thought it did tend to interfere with my peace of mind. I found myself creeping down to the workshop at three in the morning to give the gunwale a poke and try to persuade myself that that sort of dropsical sagging was exactly what you would expect on a rowing boat. At first, these nocturnal visits had an encouraging effect; any boat, after all, was solider than no boat at all. But after a while, as familiarity bred contempt, this became less helpful. In a week, I was going to have to get into a big, lethal river in her, and row for a long, long time. As this fact became more real, *Magdalen* became gauzier and less substantial. Finally, after a night of no sleep at all, I marched across to the workshop. The morning sun was playing through the workshop windows, shining through *Magdalen*'s bottom and producing an attractive dappled effect on the floor below.

Willie had followed me. He was leaning against a trestle, examining the scene with interest. 'It looks like a church,' he said.

'What looks like a church?'

'On the floor.'

It did. The shadows were not unlike those of Perpendicular tracery.

'Can churches float?' asked Willie, direct and to the point as ever.

'Not always,' I said, in a final attempt to save face. Then I went and telephoned Martin, the carpenter.

Martin arrived later that morning. He scowled briefly, scratched his dense black hair, set his jigsaw going, and cut out a perfect set of new planks for the damaged right-hand side. Due to the danger of springing, we decided to nail them on top of the old ones, using copper nails and the good old double-hammer technique which is as old as nails themselves. Two hammerers are required, both musical if possible. Man number one creeps underneath the upturned boat. Man number two drills a hole down through plank and rib, navigating by the shouted directions of his oppo. The oppo, having removed the sawdust from his eyes, watches the nail come down, waiting for the shout of 'Flush'. Now comes the complicated part.

Are you ready? roars number one, in his dusty echo chamber.

I think so, says number two, indecisively.

Okay, says number one. *Two bars waltz time with a one-bar count-in: a-ONE two three, CRASH crash crash, CRASH crash crash*. (The crashing being the thunder of hammers, one on the nail's head and the other turning the point over into the rib.)

It is a sound technique, but by no means foolproof. This is because the outside man needs an almost superhuman sense of rhythm and a hammer-arm of steel; and also because the inside man is stone deaf after the second nail. It does, however, bring a note of Viennese elegance to the workshop.

Eventually I went and lay under the boat and there was perfect blackness.

Painting a boat used to be easy. You bought paint, blue or white according to what was in the shop, and you sloshed it on. Later, you sandpapered away as many of the drips as you happened to notice and sloshed on another coat. The following years you repeated the operation. A well-painted boat had a sort of blurred look, its outlines striving to make themselves visible through an inch of paint.

It is far more difficult now. The hearts of oak, pitch, oakum and tallow days are gone from us and we shall not see their like again. Now there is hard bilge paint, soft bilge paint, antifouling, anti-fouling primer, self-etching anti-fouling primer, primer, clear primer, undercoat, overcoat and probably morning coat as well, to name but a few. The man in the chandlery looks up from his calculator, whose screen bears a sum ending in four noughts, and says. 'What do you want?'

'Some paint,' you say, nervously.

''Son the shelf,' says the chandler.

'I was wondering . . . that is, I've got a boat and I just wanted sort of basic white paint.'

The chandler's thumb makes a spastic leap on the calculator, and the light goes out. 'Now look what you done, I'll have to cash up me day's profits all over again.' He sighs. 'Your boat metal, concrete, or glass?'

'Wood, actually.'

The calculator falls to the floor with a tinkle of breaking chips. 'Wood? *Wood*? wotgermean, wood? 'Ere, Malc! Bloke here wants some wood paint!'

And the artificers file out of the workshops, reeking of petrol and resin catalyst, and stand in a horseshoe and stare at you. And you walk towards the shelf and your head hits a low beam and not wishing to make a scene you continue on your hands and knees. And twenty minutes later, you leave carrying six tins of stuff that might or might not be paint. Certainly it is impossible to tell from the labels, which seem to consist mainly of dire warnings.

The caulker, for instance, is *Danger – corrosive*. The primer is dangerous because it is hydrocarbons and on contact with water causes gassing (gassing? Poor old Uncle Alfred reeling back from Wipers with his lungs rotted to Stilton?) and the undercoat – well, it took a goodish while to get round to the undercoat, because when I had finished slapping on the primer, I felt so terrific. D'licious smell. For some reason the workshop had developed two extra doors. I tried to leave by the one on the right and injured myself by walking into a brick wall. If that is what the primer's like, I remember thinking, what about the gloss? Probably see Buddha.

On 1 October, *Magdalen* lay in the centre of the shed and gleamed. Her hull looked as if it had been dipped in milk; round her top strake ran a band of royal blue; across her nose was a brilliant blue half-deck, ostensibly to keep the rain off objects stowed below it but actually to reinforce her bow section, which was rotten to the core. Reverently, I stepped towards her. On the floor surrounding her, tiny gumboot prints in blue and white and egg-yellow undercoat danced merry sarabands. The paint had dried hard, smoothing over the mess of plastic padding and caulking compound beneath. But would she float? Karen and I jockeyed her out of the door and on to the trailer. We set off into Shropshire, turned into the gates of the gravel pit and dropped her in. (I say 'dropped'; actually she weighed about 600 pounds unladen, and it was virtually impossible to lift her far enough to drop her.) She sank. Willie and Martin cheered. I left her on the bottom; the water would work its way into her timbers and she would swell up and become watertight. That was the idea, anyway.

As we left the gravel pit, I noticed that we were being watched. High on a cliff of sand, three men were standing. Two of them were shaking their heads, not so much in disagreement as in disbelief. The third kept going away and returning a few seconds later, rubbing his eyes as if confirming to himself that he was not dreaming. They came and asked what was going on. I told them I was off to London. They backed away nervously, heads still shaking . . .

But there was no time to persuade them of my sanity. The boat was a mere container. I had to fill it with stuff.

The basic requirements were me, and a pair of oars. To this I added a spare pair of rowlocks, as a guarantee against losing the original pair (it is noticeable that as soon as you leave spares at home, the existing set loses no time in deep-sixing itself). Shelter would be provided by my excellent Bukta tent, a twelfth-birthday gift and the identical one that had burned in the Bure disaster. It had been mended since; nonetheless, its best friend would not have called it waterproof. So I purchased a bargain fly-sheet in an attractive shade of blue. I also took a sheet of builder's polythene, a Second World War officer's-issue camp-bed, and two sleeping bags (one a veteran of my first and last scout camp as well as the Bure disaster), to be used one inside the other. For cooking I took a Camping Gaz stove; for lighting, a Camping Gaz lamp.

Food was a bit of a problem. While I had heard rumours that the parts of England through which I was to pass contained a certain number of public houses, there was no way of telling whether the diet of the region would feature missionary or steak-in-a-basket, or either. Neither was actually tremendously appealing. My previous limited experience of camping had featured rather a lot of baked beans and sausages charred to perfection. This was not the correct diet for weeks of hard physical exertion in hostile country, dogged by the awesome spectre of scurvy. I became desperate, filling large plastic boxes with muesli and purchasing rattling pots of dehydrated chemical soup. Then the answer was vouchsafed to me by a friend who knew a chap who was sailing in a round-the-world single-handed race. The single-hander was apparently subsisting entirely on something called Food Pouches. There exists in Glasgow an organization known as Stevens Leafield, which as far as I know consists of a master chef surrounded by scientists who, as soon as the chef knocks up something really exceptional, seize it from him and put it in foil bags, under vacuum. This keeps it edible for a long as you like. The hungry traveller merely slaps the bag in boiling water for seven minutes, whips it out, and devours it. It is the easiest way I have yet discovered of taking a three-star restaurant with you into the hidden corners of the universe. (The muesli, I am delighted to say, festered in the bilges and was later fed to dogs.)

In addition to this lot, I took some clothes and a few things that presented themselves as indispensable, such as pair of dark glasses, a guitar, a fishing-rod, tape-recorder, mobile library, catapult, thing for taking stones out of horses' hooves, and Ford Cortina rear-view mirror in case of oarsman's neck.

It was painfully obvious, in the early days of October, that I was going to need to keep things dry; not only was it raining, but the boat leaked like a basket. Polythene bags get holes in them, and I could not face the social aspect of purchasing Tupperware. I therefore visited a nearby jam factory, where I secured a fifty-gallon plastic container with a screw top. This container was completely waterproof, but had originally been used as a receptacle for strawberries. There were a few still in it when I washed it out – white and ghostly things that stank of chemicals.

From the jam works I also acquired a water breaker, a

five-gallon plastic *bidon* which had originally held cola syrup. I washed it out twenty times, using bleach. But the five gallons, if the label was to be believed, had supplied flavour and colour for some fifteen thousand bottles of Coke and was not about to give up now. Ah, well, I thought, perhaps it would wear away with time.

The second and third (and fourth, as it happened) of October were a continual scuttle from workshop to telephone, collecting equipment and maps and filling in proposals for bigger and better life insurances at the insistence of my dependants, who also lost no time in pointing out to me the large number of weirs on the rivers. The day before I was to leave I went to the gravel pit to collect *Magdalen*, feeling sure she would be watertight by now. I pulled her out, and pumped out the water. She sank again immediately. I simply took her home, deciding it was too late to delve into the truth of the matter. It could only be depressing.

Since I was by now finding it impossible to sleep I took to getting up early and counting omens. These were uniformly unsatisfactory: pigeons flew east, owls screeched on roof trees and magpies appeared singly. The road in front of my feet was carpeted with black cats. Whenever I went upstairs someone was coming down, and the knives were always crossed at dinner. On the Sunday before my departure, the day after a pleasant dinner party for thirteen people, the back door of the car flew open, precipitating three hundredweights of mixed luggage into the A49. It really began to seem as if it might be as well to dive under a bus there and then, and spare oneself the agony of waiting. But rural bus services in Shropshire have reached a level of infrequency which offers you a better chance of being dispatched by an erupting volcano than by a bus. Besides, I was beginning to sense that there might after all be a bright side. What I was about to do would open a new page in the annals of human experience, or anyway it would make a change from digging the garden, the alternative at this time of year. It was not productive to regard it as a manifestation of the death wish.

As I collected up the last of my equipment from the workshop, I watched Willie and Martin doing carrot printing on an old sail, using carrots and boat paint. One day they would sit at my knee as I unfolded the long, slow yarn; they would thrill to the rush of weirs, weep during the long mellow courses of the canals. They would also, by the look of them, still be bright boat-blue. Sighing, I reached for a rag and some turpentine.

A lone figure, black against the drifting snowflakes, pulling into the grey clouds that press down on the wintry earth. On either side of the canal, industrial ruins lie bound in the iron frost. The black ribbon of water loses its sheen; crystals of ice form, then pancake ice, then floes. The boat slows and halts. A solitary Adélie penguin is dying of hunger between two nearby slag-heaps. Soot and snowflakes close me in . . . Lost. Lost without trace.

CHAPTER TWO

Welshpool to Shrewsbury

Henry at Welshpool – An Arthurian farewell – An enormous life-jacket – How to row upstream without a map – Life on the edge – My character is strengthened – Breidden Hill – The border – A night under canvas – Hip-deep in the midden – Squire Mytton's hiccups cure – The fornication of Irish swans – Nature notes – Shrewsbury School – The bearers of Shrewsbury Weir – Shrewsbury Sewage Farm – An enormous pike

The valley of the Severn at Welshpool has the reputation of being the wettest place in Wales. I have no statistical confirmation of this fact, and I do not know anyone who lives there and possesses a rain gauge. But Henry Gillette, driving his battered Transit van at seventy-six miles an hour down the lanes, said so, and Henry is an authority. In the back of the van lay *Magdalen*, among piles of sheep dung. A fine grey drizzle lashed at the windscreen. We turned off the road at the bridge where I had pulled the canoe out the previous night. Henry stared gloomily at the Severn, flowing sluggishly under the box girder. 'Glad it's not me going,' he said.

We pulled *Magdalen* out, dusted off the worst of the wool and filthy straw, and dragged her down to the water's edge. Henry dropped his side on a stone. 'Sorry,' he said.

'That's all right,' I assured him.

My shoulders ached slightly; the previous day I had done the long paddle in the canoe from Llanidloes. I was very tired, and nervous to the point where I was experiencing a sort of gibbering between the ears. Would she float?

'Will she float?' asked Henry. Henry looks a bit like Peter Cushing after ten years on a hill farm, combining Dracula-like gloom with weather-beatenness to an astonishing degree.

'Of course she will,' I said. 'Heave.'

Magdalen slid in a stately manner into the rain-pocked water. Henry stared into her bottom. 'Gawd,' he said. 'Leaks a bit.' Brown teardrops formed at the edges of her planks. They ran and joined. 'She'll be full in an hour,' said Henry. 'You sure about this?'

'Of course I am,' I said without conviction, slamming in the floorboards. 'Pass me some of that gear.'

'Seems an awful lot of stuff,' said Henry. 'Hadn't you better leave some of it behind?'

This time I made no reply, because I was wondering what the hell I was going to do if *Magdalen* sank. I decided that whatever happened, I was not going to sit and listen to Henry. Muttering a prayer, I locked down the bottom boards and started piling in the equipment: first the plastic buckets full of muesli, then the container (you will hear more of that damned container) and then the other junk, topped off with a beautiful yellow fish box bearing lettering to the effect that it was the property of Donegal Coop Fisheries, Killybegs, Co. Donegal.

Pulling on my waterproof trousers, I leaped in and pushed off. *Magdalen* settled low in the water, rocking. The iron bridge wheeled slowly above my head, the current took hold and Henry, a tall, stooped figure in a tattered Barbour jacket, began to shrink. As I settled the oars and took the first stroke, he waved. I noticed that he was simultaneously shaking his head. It was a moving moment; a valedictory was required. None sprang to mind, except:

> And slowly answer'd Arthur from the barge:
> 'The old order changeth, yielding place to new,
> And God fulfils himself in many ways . . .'

This, spoken as it was by the dying King Arthur disappearing towards the island valley of Avilion, seemed a bit gloomy. But I shouted it anyway, because Henry looked a bit like Sir Bedivere wondering if he could wade out far enough to get Excalibur back from the lake once old Arthur was round the corner, and pawn it.

The formalities concluded, I took stock of my position. *Magdalen* was low in the water. Telltale lapping noises emanated from under her bottom boards. The thwart upon which I was sitting was hard, and getting harder. As yet all rowlocks were in their places and all oars were unbroken, which was encouraging but not, after only five minutes of travelling, remarkable. The life-jacket was, troublesome, of course. I had borrowed it from a friend, Tim 'Short' Paganini. Paganini's nickname is a product of his stature, as you have probably guessed. I am six foot two; Paganini is six foot seven, and he had said the life jacket was too big for him. I considered taking it off and sitting on it, thereby solving at a stroke the hardness of the thwart and the sensation of being a size-six foot starting a marathon in a size-eight running shoe. But I had promised the wife, little ones, and insurance agent. The jacket stayed on. I began looking for the map.

Originally, I had decided that in the interests of science, I should not take maps but should make my own. As in all forms of human activity, concern for survival had soon overtaken purism, and I had commenced the journey with a good sheaf of Ordnance Surveys in the inside pocket of my oilskins. I now proceeded to run through them, searching for the Shrewsbury sheet, across which I was currently creeping. It was not there. Fingers shaking, I re-searched. Not a sign of it. During a preliminary inspection I seemed to remember having seen weirs on the river. In fact I *certainly* remembered seeing weirs. Without it, how would I know they were coming? The map had to be there . . .

No, it wasn't. It was on the front seat of the lorry, where I had left it, travelling south at Henry's regulation seventy-six miles per hour. But perhaps he had not started yet, and was still standing on the bridge mulling over my moving rendition of what I could remember of the *Idylls of the King*. Digging my left oar into the water, I turned round and began to row upstream.

The Severn in its upper reaches is an unimpressive-looking river. Scarcely more than a brook, really; a child of ten could throw a fair-sized boulder across it without difficulty. Or so I had thought, sailing down with wind and current, drifting in effortless silence. As I turned, however, peculiar things began to happen. The water, having previously limited itself to the odd cooing gurgle, rushed under the stem with a throaty and dangerous roar. The breeze, which had given a slight and pleasing slant to the drizzle, whipped the wavelets to hissing foam. The

[33]

oars, hitherto useful for steering but otherwise largely decorative, turned into unsympathetic baulks of timber that flayed the hands. The weight of the boat tripled. The banks of the river ceased to unreel with the calm assurance of a look-at-life travelogue, and stopped dead in their tracks. Then, inch by inch, *they started to go backwards*. Sweat poured from under my hat. I was rowing upstream. But row as I might, this stripling brook was carrying me down.

At this point a lanky figure stepped on to a gravel beach downstream. It was Henry, and he was waving the map. I collected it without stopping (actually I could not stop, because of the current). I heard him say, 'Are you *sure* about this?' I was not, but the current swept me on down the rapids. As I went, I checked the map. There were no weirs. I began to feel a bit ashamed of all the panic.

Soon the rapids grew less rapid, and I was moving down a long, placid pool lined with willows dabbling their fingers in the water. This was more like it. The water grew slower as the pool turned a corner. Ahead, lorries were roaring over what must be a bridge. Funny. There was no bridge on the map. I turned in my seat to look. Fifteen yards downstream, the river disintegrated over a two-foot wall. The roaring was not lorries, but water.

The human nervous system is a wonderful thing. One second I was seated in the boat, half-buried in Camping Gaz stoves, guitars, and mooring ropes. The next I was twenty yards away on a boulder, hanging on to a towline at the far end of which, in midstream, the laden *Magdalen* was wallowing hysterically towards the fall. On either side of my boulder, mighty waters roared. Ten feet downstream from me was another boulder. I decided to jump for it, by which time the boat would be over the sill and with a spot of luck coming to rest among the eddies below, still attached to the line.

At this point, *Magdalen* hit a rock in the middle of the weir, heeled over at an angle of forty-five degrees and stuck. I changed my mind about jumping.

This was *the moment* – the reason for the whole expedition. A

moment with *finality potential*, where one tin
bring the whole edifice down in a pile of
ultimately, *here and now*. During the philoso
had brought the grand design to maturit
apparent that these moments were the parts of the expe
most likely to contribute to my spiritual development. Decisions
would have to be accurate and correct. There was no room for
shilly-shallying; consciousness and action would have to move as
one, as in Zen archery. I had been looking forward to moments
like these, and was prepared to savour them to the last drop.

Now one had happened, though, I experienced a spiritual pang,
wishing that here and now were elsewhere and at a more convenient time. As I leaned back on the towrope and watched my
spare gas cartridges spill into the roaring foam, powerful curses
spewed between my clenched teeth. *Magdalen* shifted uneasily and
swung over the weir. I did not see this because I had been taken
unawares by the sudden lurch and had therefore stepped backwards into three foot six of water, which was surprisingly cold
for the time of year. I am unable to tell you its exact temperature
because before I could whip out the thermometer the strain came
back on the rope, jerking me down to the next boulder. I
progressed down the northern side of the weir as though
waterskiing, coming to rest in a clump of weeds. *Magdalen*
became involved in a back-eddy and glided towards me, nuzzling
at my boot like an affectionate dog. I drew back my boot to kick
her. Then I thought, no, it was not her fault. So I sort of stroked
her shamefacedly with my toe, and bailed her out with the
saucepan. Twenty minutes later, we were back on the river again.

After that, I kept the map in an inside pocket and did not refer
to it. There were no further weirs, but there were times when the
river ran close to the road. The sound of a heavy lorry caused me
to shy like a startled horse. It still does.

The Severn clings to its youth like a Californian dowager,
scarcely increasing in width until it escapes from Wales,
presumably afraid that someone will tax it or steal it, two

vourite Welsh occupations. It fairly rips along, first north-
easterly and then due east for Shrewsbury. Trees and islands of
debris lie in the water, green twigs jittering with a sound like a
muffled line-printer with the pull of the stream. The banks are
high; all you can see is the sky, some tall trees and Breidden Hill, a
lofty outcrop of rock studded with wrecked hang-gliders and
surrounded with tall radio masts. It was pleasant to have something to look at. There was something rather sublime about those
aerials, too, more than five hundred feet above the ground. The
mind's eye watched ant-like figures creeping out to repair a rusty
wire, careless of the awful gulf below; leaving, perhaps, a frag-
ment of a loved one's underwear as a token of a daring feat
achieved in the course of duty. It was a moving thought, and left,
as the river's winding hid the pylons from view, a sort of mellow
glow, a preparedness to appreciate fully whatever was next on the
agenda. Looking over my shoulder, I saw that it was another
pylon. Well, that was alright. Doubtless there would be three or
four more. One could put up with that; presumably they were
company for each other. As I passed under the aerial array, I
thought how very similar it was to the other one. Then I thought,
hang on, this isn't similar, it's the same one. Well, well. Perhaps
the river took a quick wiggle. On I rowed. And on, and on.

And I went under that damned aerial again, and again. And
after that again, until I lost count, because the blood was pound-
ing in my ears and I was seeing visions of oxy-acetylene cutters
and drooling. I would bet any money that that pylon had legs. As
soon as it was out of sight it sniggered for a bit and then rushed
forward, on tiptoe, to cut me off . . .

It was time to bail out again.

An old Severn hand had warned me: always find a camp spot
before dark. While I could not believe it was getting dark already,
it was hard to tell. The Welshpool Valley seems to exist in a
perpetual twilight, which varies in intensity according to the
thickness of the rainclouds interposing themselves between the
observer and the sun. Certainly, things were looking gloomy;

but the dark streaks of cloud were fairly lashing in from the Atlantic, and besides, the banks were very high.

The river ran through a lonely stretch far from roads. Snipe made noises like old men with chest infections. Sandpipers piped in a ghastly manner. Moorhens skulked in the vegetation, killing themselves with silent laughter. On the left bank Offa's Dyke glided by, soaked in ancient blood. I began to shiver. The reflections in the water passed from green to black. Night was certainly falling, now. My hands were raw. The river was getting narrower . . .

Then, all of a sudden, it doubled its width and the sky brightened. A steely evening light glittered in a wide sheet of water. I had arrived at the border and the confluence of Afon Vyrnwy, simultaneously. A group of fine black cedars stood sentinel. It was as if I had emerged from one of those Mabinogion tales full of hunting dogs and severed heads and arrived in an eighteenth-century pastoral scene. The great stream bunched under *Magdalen*'s keel and bore us on.

As night fell, I came to a farm on the north bank. I went ashore, and walked stiff-legged up to the sheds. It was cold; the cows in the milking parlour steamed. A small man with an apron made from an old fertilizer sack said I could camp in the orchard. He and his brother ran the farm. The brother had bright red cheeks and teeth spaced wide in his head like a coarse comb. They kept up a continuous stream of insults aimed at each other. (Pay no attention to him, he's always drunk; he'd be drunk but he can't hold it, look; trouble with a brother like that is he's a constant suffering to his family; trouble with a brother like that is he's never up early enough in the morning to make anything suffer; look at the state of the bloody hedges; O! he's a torment to me; O! he's a burden to carry.) They grinned at each other like mad, loving it. The yard and the orchard and the hedges were neat and crisp, the cattle well cared for.

Back in the tent, the drinking water tasted of Coca-Cola. I thought I might go and talk to the brothers some more, but I was tired. I woke often in the night, freezing cold. Rain rattled constantly on the fly-sheet, and there was an awful smell. I lay and worried about whether *Magdalen* would hold out, whether I could get over Shrewsbury Weir, and whether the brothers were mass murderers and I had camped on one of their victims' shallow graves. In the dawn, the rain fell in sheets. I crawled shuddering from the tent into a dark-grey, watery world, and blundered into a large muck heap, which explained the smell.

The light grew. The river, which yesterday had been running black and clear, was up eighteen inches and the colour and transparency of strong cocoa. I struck camp and repacked. The container was proving admirably waterproof. As I screwed it up, I caught my little finger in the thread and was unable to get it out for some minutes. I knelt whimpering over the smashed remains, trying to convince myself I had never liked that finger anyway. Then I kicked the container all the way back to the boat, to show it who was boss.

As I sloshed about in the liquid mud by the river bank, the brother with the teeth came to see me off. He looked at the writhing surface of the water, then at the boat, then at me. 'You must be . . . pretty brave,' he said. I had the distinct impression that he had been on the point of saying something a good deal less flattering, but as I had already discovered, his manners were perfect, provided you weren't related to him.

The river reflected the rolling grey clouds; it ran far from habitation, in huge shallow curves. In the eddies where the force of the current was broken by fallen trees or beaches of grey gravel, rafts of mallard waited. As I passed, they rocketed into the air in clouds of spray with a suddenness that stopped the heart. Two magpies flopped across my path as I ate breakfast on a long, slow pool. This was the first good omen I had had for some time. It was comforting to sit on the wide, shining bosom of the river and be borne onwards; comforting and curiously safe.

However, after breakfast I had to stop on a sandbar at the inside of a bend and bail fifty saucepans of water from

Magdalen's bilges. She was beginning to display a talent for keeping things in proportion.

This morning was meant to form a pattern for the days that were to follow. Having made a decent amount of progress, I would engage in some cultural activity, such as a little light exploring or a bit of tomb appreciation, before taking a substantial luncheon in a public house. In this way I should avoid the usual breakneck hurtle across the landscape, looking neither to right nor left. Unfortunately, things did not work out like that. The river was flowing at even greater speed than on the previous day. This meant that I arrived at the site of my historical project while I was still eating breakfast, and by public house opening time was making steady progress through a huge, dry, empty area marked on the map as an army firing range. The place I had meant to visit was Mytton, which presumably has links with the Squire of the same name, one of the dominant figures of the late eighteenth century. Squire Mytton is remembered for many heroic deeds, among them setting fire to his nightshirt to cure himself of hiccups, and jumping a coach-and-four over a post and rails. He died in drunken penury at Boulogne, which seems bad luck, and I really wished to intimate to his shade that in my view he had had a raw deal. Mytton was renowned for his impatience, however, so I suppose that he of all people would understand my reasons for not stopping.

This is not to say that I wasn't learning anything. For it was on this day that I first observed the sartorial perversity syndrome. In this, the rower swathes himself on starting out in oilskins and polythene, making quite sure that no part of him is exposed to the lethal downpour forecast for this morning by men in rooms without windows in Broadcasting House. The sun comes out immediately after breakfast, cooking him *en papillote*. It will rain by elevenses, he says to himself. It does not. Slowly, garment by garment, with every sign of suspicion, he unwraps. At lunchtime the sun hangs vast and golden at the meridian. He sets out the viands on a snowy tablecloth and removes his jersey. Just as the garment hits the bottom boards, black clouds sweep at terrifying speed across the sky, and the landscape disappears behind lashing sheets of rain . . .

On the previous day I had chased the whole of the Severn's swan population ahead of me. They must have camped for the night somewhere near the tent, because as I set off so did they, collecting the local swans in a sort of snowball swim.

The river had lost any claim to smallness, and was now large and powerful, flowing through savage country with wooded cliffs swooping down to black eddies and huge rapids down which the swans sailed like great ships in a tide-race.

Swans must be some of the stupidest animals alive. In the lonely places where they are not in danger, they keep miles away from humans. In more populated spots they rush towards anyone on the banks, gobbling up with pitiful eagerness the offerings of lead shot and rat poison brought by urban nature lovers. This death wish seems to extend into their mating, which I was once privileged to witness in Ireland. While fishing for salmon on a precipitous stretch of the River Blackwater, I was surprised to see a swan belting downstream with his head down, beak in the water and the soles of his feet bounding through the foam. As he came opposite me, I thought there was something wrong; the foam under his feet looked solid, and the attitude of his body strangely top-heavy. At this point there was a small eruption in the water under his nose, and something I at first thought was a large white snake put its head up and coughed, loudly. Since this was Ireland I rapidly cancelled the snake theory, and a second later a female swan emerged from the water, kicking furiously and spluttering, the male still standing on her back and jumping up and down in an aggrieved manner, as if trying to re-sink her. They had undoubtedly been having it away: you could tell by the look in her eye. I do not know if this is general swan practice. If so, it seems yet another bit of anti-feminist bad luck that the female of the swan species can only get her rocks off while holding her breath. It does, however, raise interesting questions about the Narcissus-like attitude of male swans. Since witnessing

[40]

the mating I have come to assume that they are not admiring their own reflections, but staring into the water in the hope that a bit of snicket will glide out of the gloom.

The Severn here takes a huge loop round the Isle of Grange. The stream of Llanidloes has become a sixty-yard-wide monster but the style is unchanged. Long, slow pools, steep-banked and mirror-smooth, run under wooded cliffs. In the tails of the pools, the smooth water narrows to a spearhead of looking-glass in the middle of sudden boilings and swellings of the current; then the smoothness is gone, and the water runs with a coarse rocking motion between long banks of gravel, slowing by degrees until it becomes the neck of the next pool downstream, with cormorants fishing bodilessly on the glassy current, and a salmon leaping in the shadows under a tall black wellingtonia.

By two o'clock, the river was slowing down. This was a bit nerve-racking, as the reason for the rallentando was Shrewsbury Weir. But Shrewsbury Weir was seven or eight miles away yet. It must, one was forced to conclude, be enormous.

The Army teaches people to fly helicopters on the approaches to Shrewsbury, so you are lucky if you can hear yourself think on the way in. Workmen were tearing down a row of old cottages and putting up a nice new petrol station. How much more pleasing to see little plastic pennants fluttering bravely in the breeze than a lot of horrible slimy old medieval buttresses. And how lovely to see, for the first time since the source, the merry splatter of the Terrible Pipe, hurling its effluent into the river.

Shrewsbury begins with a series of Victorian houses arranged on hills so they can peer disapprovingly at the river. These are followed by a drunken bunch of late medieval warehouses, bulging dissolutely at the seams. Just as you are expecting the serious stuff to begin, with Marks & Spencer and W. H. Smith and Woolworth's and the rest of them, the town steps briskly back from the river, its place being filled on one side by a pleasing green park, and on the other by Shrewsbury School, among whose alumni are Charles Darwin (who did not like the

[41]

place, finding the sheets damp) and John Cleese.

Pupils of the school were rowing hither and thither in small, sharp boats. Many of them seemed to be doing it for the first time, and for a while they seemed to come at us from all sides. *Magdalen* complicated the situation by getting a sudden attack of dignity, and deciding she was as good as any coxless four. While this was certainly true, it left out of account the fact that a coxless four amidships can sink a light cruiser. We battled in midstream, cursing. Eventually I got her to the side and we skulked downstream under the bank.

As we passed Shrewsbury School's boathouse, a large crowd stopped what it was doing and stared. A spokesman asked where we were going.

'London.'

Pause. 'You're on the wrong river.'

'I know.'

'And there's a weir downstream.'

'I know.'

At this point, the Shrewsbury smile started; ineffably superior but ineffably good-natured, it implied that its proprietor realized he was talking to a madman, but was too polite to acknowledge the fact. Where coarser folk shake their heads or tap their temples, Shrewsbury pupils smile.

'Nice boat,' said the smiler.

'Yes.'

'Better than this.' he said, indicating a toothpick-like sliding-seat rigger. 'More room. Sort of, well, fatter.'

'Quite,' I said. *Magdalen* lurched slightly. She had not come down from the wilds to be patronized like this. *I-am-not-fat*, she seemed to say. *I-am-not-fat*, in time to the oarstrokes.

The boathouse fell astern. The roaring began.

This roaring resembled the soundtrack from a film about the Battle of the Somme, with the intervals of silence removed. Thought-provoking.

Under the railway bridge, I could hear the Tannoy say, 'Bing bong, the train now standing at platform seven is the 4.30 for

Church Stretton. Craven Arms and Ludlow.' Ludlow is my home station. Suddenly I was acutely homesick.

'Weir' is one of those words with an unpleasant Anglo-Saxon sound to it, reminiscent of weirdness, werewolves and bewaring. No word containing this mixture of semi-consonant and diphthong could ever be pleasant or consoling. It is weirs like Shrewsbury that have given this perfectly innocent vowel-sound its present appalling reputation: a steep slope perhaps fifty yards across, with a vertical drop of twelve feet. The water goes over the top like a sheet of bent green glass (the top ten feet of Niagara Falls looks very similar). About four feet down, it goes all bubbly, as if not liking the look of the rough stuff at the bottom. But by then it is too late and it is irrevocably on its way. This does not, however, stop it trying to climb back up once it has reached the bottom. Which gives rise to what is called the 'stopper', a standing wave of water between four and six feet high, white as snow. It is the stopper that makes all the noise. Having seen the stopper, I hope I never see a starter.

Science has shown that rushing water gives off many negative ions. These are tiny charged particles that make you feel terrific, and are supposed to be the main reason that Niagara Falls is the honeymoon capital of the western hemisphere (though I have a sneaking suspicion that the motels with heart-shaped windows and blood-heat jumbo water beds may have something to do with it, too).

On this occasion the ions seemed not to be working. I was feeling far from terrific as I gazed at the mighty waters.

My scheme had been to let *Magdalen* down on the end of a rope, as I had done the previous day. It was quite obvious, however, that this would not be possible, unless I wanted her efficiently minced. On the far side of the weir there was a fish pass, a foot too narrow. On the staging at the bottom a graffiti artist, presumably faint with exhaustion, had written, THE LAW REQUIRES THAT A BOAT PASS BE PROVIDED, a sentiment with which I was in complete agreement. A lock might perhaps have been excessive. But a set of boat rollers, now. Cheap to install, easy to maintain . . . It was enough to make the mouth water.

Meanwhile, I was stuck.

There was a chap at Niagara Falls who used to stare at raging waters, too. It was in the 1820s that he arrived, an Englishman of good family, few possessions and a great but secret sorrow. He erected a little hut on Goat Island in the middle of the falls, where he kept bantams. Every day he would sit on a small jetty he had constructed towards the lip of the falls, playing a black wooden flute. As time went on, the jetty grew longer, as did the periods of time he spent sitting on it. Eventually he built a sort of spring board from it over the abyss; from its end he watched the plunging waters. Finally he took to hanging from the end of his springboard by his fingertips, with the spray buffeting his face.

And then one morning he was gone.

I knew how he must have felt. I stood and watched the weir and meditated on the futility of human existence.

A voice behind me asked where I was going and what I was up to. It belonged to a medium-sized lad in a life-jacket. He seemed to be wet, an impression confirmed by the kayak under his right arm. Having answered his questions, I asked him if he would consider helping me drag the boat over the weir. To my astonishment he agreed, summoning a companion to my assistance. They had been doing a spot of kayaking, they said, indicating the seething cross-currents. From certain hidden signs I deduced that they thought I was mad. Well, the feeling was mutual. I am sincerely grateful, as without their help I would probably still be sleeping on a bench at the top of the weir, fending off the witticisms of interested bystanders. (Gor, haven't you got a lot of stuff? Goin' to London? You're on the wrong river for that, har, har.)

The weir is a popular local beauty spot. People go there to read the evening paper and drink tea out of Thermoses, and to watch other people do dangerous things with boats. The sight of all this shameless relaxation was too much for my deep-seated organizing instinct. Barking a few orders, I arranged the transportation of my baggage the two hundred yards from the top of the weir to my re-embarkation point. Suddenly I found myself at the rear of a long line of old-age pensioners, each of whom was burdened with an oar or a bucket of cameras or a bag of muesli. Evening papers blew unattended into the river. Cups of tea cooled in the afternoon breeze. The pensioners moved with clockwork precision, dumping their loads and returning to line the railings to watch me reload.

A very pretty girl helped me put the final touches. I bailed out, and pressed a bar of chocolate on her. It would not stick. Releasing the painter, I let the current bear me away. Above the roar of the weir came a thin, heartening sound.

My loyal OAPs were cheering.

That night I pulled into the mouth of a little tributary opposite Shrewsbury Sewage Works. After I had put the tent up, I went for a walk. It was a dryish, greyish evening. On the brow of the hill behind the river a shallow ditch full of thornbushes was all that was left of the Shrewsbury Canal. A curious mood of complacency was on me, partly as a result of having conquered the legendary Shrewsbury Weir, and partly because I had broken into the half-bottle of medicinal Bell's, to considerable effect. The troubles of the world seemed small and far away.

As the red ball of the sun rolled down behind the sewage farm, I seemed to hear the cries of long-gone bargees, the hooves of straining towhorses, the creak of lock balance-beams. It would be a fine thing to cross the Heart of England on one of those lanes of still water; a peaceful process, and one allowing time for mellow reflection on the relics of vanished industries. (It is easy to deduce from this that I had never been near a canal.)

I returned to the tent through a flock of small boys who zoomed across the field like a flight of jackdaws. A man with an endless shadow was standing by *Magdalen*'s mooring, staring down into the smooth water as if he expected to see pictures in it. He told me I was camped in the best pike spot on the river, and pointed out a fifteen-pounder, huge as a log, indistinct in the darkening shelter of a dead tree. He had canoed down the river in

1940; I asked him if there was any trouble in store. He gave me to understand that there were rapids at Ironbridge; he knew a bloke when he was young, rolled over at the top of the rapids. They found him a good way downstream a week later, horribly mangled. He gave me an odd sideways look. But I should have no trouble in *that*, jerking his head at *Magdalen*. Then he faded into the night.

Later, as the gas popped in the mantle, I tried to construe that sideways look. It had had a curious menacing quality. The dangers of the Severn – the smiling farmer's hesitation over his choice of words, and now this fellow – seemed to have rather efficient press agents. Of course people loved to exaggerate these things. Load of rubbish, more than likely . . .

Still, the pike had been real.

But next morning the pike, huge as a log, actually was a log.

CHAPTER THREE

Shrewsbury to Bewdley

Altitude sickness in Shrewsbury – A gaggle of cavalry officers – Two local Webbs – Enter the Severn Gorge – The pious Darbys – The impious John Wilkinson – Down the rapids and into civilization – How to drag a barge up the white water – The high priests of the angle – The further march of civilization – The spirit of the Midlands – Horribly mangled – Reflections on micturition – The world of bungalows – Hot Coke in Bewdley

On the morning of the fourth day, I was woken by the smell of artificial strawberries, courtesy of the container. I was feeling rather groggy, and not only because of the strawberries. Testing my symptoms – aching head, disinclination to move, penetrating urge to go back to sleep – I decided I had a slight case of altitude sickness. This was mysterious, Shrewsbury being only a couple of hundred feet above sea level. Probably it was because I was sleeping in a tent. Nonetheless, as I went through the preliminary motions of getting up, I had the feeling that something was wrong. The first light of dawn was shining on the tent roof. Reeling to the tent entrance, I looked out. (It is not easy to reel on all fours, but altitude sickness and a small tent are good teachers.) The dawn was not dawn but the lights of Shrewsbury, and the clock said 1 a.m. Reeling back into the tent, I reeled into my sleeping bag and reeled down into oblivion.

Magdalen seemed to contain less water than usual when I bailed her out that morning. I started at first light, waking the swans (many of which had preceded us over Shrewsbury Weir, marching solemnly in line ahead.) The swans took up their positions, I dug deep with the oars and we commenced, under a clear sky still delicately flushed with the dawn.

The river below Shrewsbury enters a flat, empty land. The morning mists hung grey over the water, and occasional fishermen sat throned under banks pocked with sand-martin holes. We ·drifted quietly, watching mallard skulking in corners, and trying to pretend that we were not, at bottom, scared by the Severn Gorge.

The current whirled us under Atcham Bridge, trying to crush

us against the piers. But we were getting cunning now, and knew how to steer. Below Atcham, ploughed meadows stretched depressingly to the horizon; the silence was total.

Not quite.

From round a bend there came the sound of thousands of cavalry officers waiting for the bar to open at a hunt ball. But it was the wrong time of day for a hunt ball. Could it be a sponsored swim in aid of the regimental polo fund? Or even a rehearsal for the Third World War? I waited with bated breath for the roar of diesels and the chug of heavy machine-guns. The conversation continued. I rounded the bend. The river was full of submarines, their periscopes up. Every single periscope turned on me. By now thoroughly disorientated, I smiled politely, said, 'Excuse me,' and caught a crab. As the spray cleared, the sky darkened, full of huge objects. It was like the fly-past at Farnborough Air Show. *And still the conversation continued.* It was terrible . . .

It was Canada geese. There must have been a thousand of them, gone native after absconding from somebody's ornamental gaggle. I was lucky not to have been eaten alive, or anyway fanned to death by their wings. When I had my elevenses, it was with a hand that shook.

Towards lunchtime, the hills began to rise ahead. The Severn was still a salmon river, pool and run, the current ripping under low cliffs of red Shropshire earth, banks of gravel rising like whales from the inside of the bends. But when I looked over my shoulder I could see the Wrekin, a plum-pudding-shaped hill crowned with aerials, and a sharp indentation in the hills that climbed behind it. On the southern side of the notch in the hills, the tall stacks of Ironbridge power station spewed white smoke at the sky. I was sitting on the life-jacket, the hardness of the wooden seat having overcome my scruples about safety. But now I put it on.

Ten minutes later I took it off again, because the hills were still five miles away. *Magdalen* ploughed the water with offensive solidity. It was not, she wished me to understand, her custom to overreact.

We were passing through Webb country.

The Webbs in question are twain, as far as I know unrelated, and would certainly have found difficulty in discovering common ground. I refer, of course, to the novelist and poet Mary Webb, and Captain John Webb. Mary wrote tales in which dark purple human emotions tangle with dense Shropshire undergrowth. Captain Webb learned to swim by falling at an early age into the Severn Gorge. He subsequently commanded a merchant ship, taking advantage of his proximity to water to cover great distances at a snappy crawl; became famous for being the first man to swim the English Channel; and perished while trying to swim the whirlpool below Niagara Falls. It is popularly supposed that this was because of the lethal currents there; my personal theory, having visited the place and sniffed it, is that he swallowed a mouthful of water, was poisoned and sank. Mary Webb lived in obscurity, becoming famous after her death thanks to the admiration of Stanley Baldwin. Captain Webb, extremely famous during his lifetime, now looks merely a loony in a peculiar bathing suit. Poor old Mary. Poor old Captain.

The Severn Gorge comes on you suddenly. One moment you are in the wide, rolling valley of the agricultural Severn. The next, you are passing under Buildwas Bridge and the valley sides are right on top of you, rising steeply from the water's edge, matted with bramble and ivy and slender second-growth trees. The mat of vegetation swells with half-visible shapes. Here and there a corner of brickwork shoulders through, a relic of a time when the gorge was the heart of British manufacturing. The physical landscape here still gives clues to the violent surges of capitalism that altered its geology. The hills are honeycombed with pits and tunnels; beside the river, the constantly eroding banks are as likely to be blast-furnace slag and smashed tiles as natural gravel.

Constricted by the hills, the river has a feeling of pressure, like a steam-boiler riding its safety valve. It is black in colour; the banks overhang, crowded with trees and ruined buildings, and an early horse-railway built out on brick brackets. Even the

[51]

cooling towers of Ironbridge power station seem to be built over, rather than beside, the water.

The gorge is in constant motion. The roads alongside it and in the short, steep valleys leading down to the river stretch like chewing-gum, buckling and cracking with the movement of the earth. It is a funnel in which everything moves: men and money, machines and coal; boats up the inclined plane, clay to the pottery, and iron ore to the furnaces; eroded rock down to the river; and the water, piled high, looking for the line of least resistance, howling for the sea.

The gorge changes the Severn. Not only the scenery, but the purpose of the river, and the nature of it. Agriculture is all upstream, now. The gorge drags a boat into the Industrial Revolution and shoots it on a flume of water into the modern world.

The Severn Gorge is the northern extremity of the eighteenth-century equivalent of the M1. Two hundred years ago, a hundred and fifty barges were plying downstream to Bristol loaded with cast- and wrought-iron, or returning dragged up the rapids by teams of fifty to eighty men.

The subject of De Loutherbourg's painting, *Coalbrookdale by Night,* a picture which confirms everybody's worst fears about the early Industrial Revolution, is beside the gorge. Those were the days when coal and iron ore were part of a farmer's crop, like corn or cattle. The Darbys came up from Bristol, found they could smelt iron with coke instead of charcoal, and set up big furnaces blown by water-wheels and atmospheric engines. They discovered economies of scale. The working classes laboured in conditions so like hell that the revivalist preachers had nothing left to threaten them with. The ironmasters paid them and housed them and kept them drunk. Many of the ironmasters, such as the Darbys, were Quakers, who started turning out cauldrons by the thousand to finance the very un-Quakerish 'triangular trade'. In the triangular trade, Bristol slavers exchanged cauldrons for slaves in West Africa, and sold the slaves for money or sugar or tobacco in the West Indies or America. Then they took their profits and came back for more cauldrons. The Darbys were heavy, serious people, and good Quakers, provided it did not cut into the profits. They made guns, too. And they built the first iron bridge in the world, high above the Severn Gorge. It is not only the first; it must also be the most elegant. And it must be one of the few bridges in the world that has a new town called after it.

John Wilkinson had fewer scruples than the Darbys, but seems to have been better liked. He managed to get his house burned down by patriotic mobs for casting Republican aspersions on the Church and the King. He was a terrible bodger – having bought licences to manufacture Boulton and Watt patent steam engines for his own use, he let his mechanics put the things together so badly that the inventors wanted to withdraw the licences, on the grounds that he was bringing the product into disrepute.

But bodgers are also inventors.

Wilkinson got a blacksmith to knock up an iron barge, the *Trial*, riveted like a boiler. Nothing like it had ever been seen before. It stood to reason that boats had to be made of wood. Everyone told him it would sink. It floated. He was delighted, not so much because of the boat (one suspects) as because he had shown the buggers. During shortages of coin of the realm, he simply minted his own. And when he died, having quarrelled with just about everybody he had ever met, he was buried in an iron coffin. He left an estate valued at the phenomenal sum of £120,000. He had been a keen concubinist, at least partly because he reckoned that fornication was a sovereign cure for indigestion (he once cured his mistress of a near-fatal attack between courses at a dinner party). As a result, he had many children, legitimate and otherwise. They fought over the money like ferrets, and when they had finished, there was nothing left.

The gorge had its heyday in the Napoleonic Wars. After that, markets shrank, mines were worked out, the railways took over from the waterways, and the world lost interest. So the great machine, the horse-powered railways and man-hauled barges, De Loutherbourg's fire-limned waggon and its gin-sodden carter, the cauldrons and guns and sash windows and bridges, ran down. It was a slow decline – Coalbrookdale did not touch bottom until the 1930s. Now, it is even pretty, or at any rate prettier than Telford, the new town to its north. Some of the buildings and furnaces are still visible from the river: the weirdly castellated malt house; some artisans' dwellings, spindly and rickety-looking, constructed of red brick that has a scorched look, as if left too close to the great flames of the blast furnaces.

Two hundred yards below the Ironbridge, the white horses were jumping.

I had meant to submit the lower half of the Severn Gorge to a pretty searching scrutiny, commenting at length on aspects of ironworks financing, ore grade and value, and the products of the Jackfield and Coalport ceramic manufactories. Unfortunately, the water was moving too fast and in too many directions simultaneously, including upwards. I passed down the steepish slope at what felt like forty miles an hour and might have been ten, spinning like a top. Then there was a giant power line with pylons, and the hills stood back from the river, and the wilds lapped down to the banks again. And there we were; four days out, ninety miles from the start, drifting through a place where no roads came down to the river. After the roar of the gorge, the silence was thick and heavy. *Magdalen* swung in an eddy, watched by cows, and slid under a bridge overlooked by Apley Court, a castellated pile that could have been an original for Blandings Castle. I began to wonder if this was all really happening. It seemed most implausible that I was being borne on this huge, wild river through what is actually a fairly heavily built up area. There was a strong element of magic in the whole business; I could have been invisible, or travelling in the fifth dimension. Looking upstream at a reach down which I had travelled, I thought I saw a dirty figure in a small white rowing boat, shaking its head and thinking that there was a strong element of magic in the whole business . . .

But then a cow mooed at me, and since the river was moving easily and the water was clean, I decided to shave. Being of a fairly solitary disposition, I was not exactly lonely; but I remember thinking it would be nice to talk to *someone*, even if only to confirm that I was actually visible. The face in the mirror was a

[54]

bluish, bristly barbarian, with food all over it. Watched by the mildly curious cows, I removed the undergrowth to the point where, I calculated, I no longer inspired horror. Then I squared my shoulders at the oars and pulled with a new briskness.

The navigation of the upper Severn is a tribute to human muscle power. Nowadays the limit of navigation is at Bewdley, some miles downstream from the gorge. Once, the barges went all the way up to Pool Quay and beyond. Pool Quay is nearly at Welshpool, miles of rapids and shallows from the sea.

Rivers are kept up with weirs, which dam up the water to make it deep enough for boats to float. Weirs are usually found in association with locks – all pound locks nowadays, with a gate at either end and sluices you crank up and down to fill or empty them. These are a fairly recent invention; they are also astonishingly expensive to build. A cheaper, more primitive and generally coarser solution is the flash lock.

To build an impromptu flash lock you need about eighty men and a river. A boat is optional, serving the purpose of providing a reason for building the lock in the first place. The boat, if used, is towed as far up the river as current and depth allow. When it grinds to a halt, the men collect rocks and trees and, in the case of the rougher crews, cottages and farm carts, and bung them into the river to form a dam. It is a very rapid river that falls a foot in a mile; so if you can raise the water level two feet, you gain plenty of ground. Travelling upstream, you have to wait for the river to back up. Travelling downstream, you cruise up to your dam and break it down. The resulting lump of water is known as the 'flash', and the idea is to stay aboard it until the diverging banks have lowered it to the point where you are bumping the bottom again.

On most of the waterways of England, horses were the motive power. On the Severn, however, human beings were used, because they did not need a towpath and also because it was found that horses made lousy flash weirs, at least when alive. This caused terrible suffering to people of conscience, and many efforts were made to relieve the poor man-haulers. These were eventually successful, at which the first towpath between

Gloucester and Shrewsbury was built. The man-haulers rioted with horrible violence. Nobody had consulted them, and it transpired that they looked on the whole thing as an excuse to be paid for getting some fresh air, not to mention money, rum, pheasants, wenches and anything else not nailed down by the riverside. But as usual, nobody paid any attention to them. So one meets few, if any, on the Severn now.

Modern civilization next revealed itself in the guise of a fisher-man. He was a foxy-faced individual, dressed in Lincoln green and looking like one of Robin Hood's merrie men who had gulped down one of the King's deer and was now experiencing acute indigestion. He shouted pettishly, instructing me to keep to the far side of the river so as not to disturb the fish. This I did, thinking that the brotherhood of the angle is a firm fellowship bound together by invisible chains stronger than steel. It was at this point that I ran into a willow tree, sustaining severe abrasions to the limbs and torso. The merrie man must have seen it, and misdirected me out of sheer spite. I have always been a keen fan of Izaak Walton, in whose considered opinion anglers are honest men. The behaviour of this lizard-coloured little brute was therefore disillusioning.

At that early stage, however, it was possible to identify with him a little. Those of us who have fallen victim to the deadly addiction of fishing know the ease with which the quarry is put off its food. If you haven't caught anything for eight hours and it has been raining all day, the lowing of a cow three fields away can bring on an attack of murderous rage. Why cannot the bloody thing keep quiet, you mutter, chewing desperately at the cork handle of your rod. It is ruining the fishing by making that appalling noise. But when the fish are biting, herds of cattle can rampage down the middle of the river playing percussion instruments, and you are pleased to see them, snapping your fingers to their infectious rhythm. On the River Wye it is even accepted that in order to wake the fish up and stimulate their appetites, the angler's dog should be encouraged to swim across the pool. (In earlier times, the wife did the swimming; this state of affairs is now, happily, dead – as indeed were many of the wives, particularly if they were involved in this ritual during the spring fishing).

The procession above Bridgnorth contained at least fifty anglers. While some were dressed in the regulation green drab, many others were clad in 1980s-style space angler gear, designed for the more convenient massacre of half-inch roachlets. This consists of a peaked cap as worn by American truck drivers; dark glasses, Polaroid, preferably aviator-style; brilliant red Match Kings T-shirt, green apron with kangaroo pocket (pocket filled with maggots), PVC miniskirt to protect bum from wetness and gratify plastic fetish if any; and thigh waders, worn with Captain Blood turnovers (it is not etiquette to get your thigh waders wet). The basket containing the gear is about twelve cubic feet of wickerwork, containing reels, line, floats, weights, lunch, tea, beer, whisky, fags, litter for distribution, knife for carving name on trees, lavatory paper to mark carsey site in riverside woods, and in really advanced cases Jam tapes for Sony Walkman. And all this wondrous gear, used in conjunction with a fat holdall of rods, a keepnet, landing-net, and umbrella, is designed specifically for the torture of fish which you can't even eat. Though it must be said, in all fairness, that this lot of anglers was not indulging in much fish torture. Only one man claimed to have caught a fish. Sixty per cent of the others told me, with wry grins, that they had large sums of money staked on their expectation of weighing in with the lightest catch. Then, showing further evidence of an irrepressible sense of humour, they told me (as I sped by on the spate) that it wouldn't be so easy comin' oop.

I was at first in some confusion as to whether fishing is a religion or a disease. The jokes clinched it; definitely a religion. It has most of the requirements: a belief in blind luck, whose workings become evident (but never plain) to the initiate; a Deity, associated with but not identical to gravity, which causes rivers to flow and groundbait to sink; a sacrament, being the maggot, vouchsafed to the fishy tribe in the form of groundbait but concealing, in some cases, a hook ('many are called, but few are chosen'); Heaven, Hell, and Judgement (the Keepnet of the

[57]

Lord; the Lord's Damaged Fish; the Returning to the Water when the keepnet shall be opened at the Last Weigh-in); and a Form of Words, comparable to Christian collects – the Joke or Jokes of the Day. There is also a tremendous volume of Scripture, divided into the Old Testament (the Lonsdale and Badminton libraries, Izaak Walton, and the *Treatise on Fysshynge with an Angle*) and a New Testament (Richard Walker on still-water fly fishing, and the new evangelists of bleak-bashing, quivertipping and goz-zerzooming).

If this seems absurd, consider the facts. Anglers very seldom catch fish. Yet they sit hour after hour staring into murky water and displaying no signs of life, except occasionally to caress their maggots or, with a flick of the hand not unlike that used by a censing altar-boy, to fling another handful near their float. I strongly suspect that those hunched figures with the funny hats are contemplating the Great Analogies against the day when the Hook of the Lord will remove them from the Swim of Life and deposit them, using the Landing-net of Grace, in the Aquarium of the Chosen.

They also serve who only sit and wait.

Once the fishermen had started the rot, civilization approached rapidly and depressingly. The air was full of the heavy, pre-thunderstorm quality that signals the proximity of the Midlands proper. Children jeered from Bridgnorth Bridge. Luckily we were going too fast for their spit.

Below Bridgnorth (an Italian city, perched on a high rock) the river did its best to undo the work of civilization. It was extremely wide, extremely deep, and hurtling along at a great pace. This was a little disturbing, but I had cause to be grateful for it as I approached Quatford. The day's intense historical research had left me rather exhausted, and I had intended to camp there. As I approached, however, my nostrils were assailed by the mingled reek of chip fat and sewage. Soon afterwards, civilization commenced in the shape of a caravan site that ran alongside the river for nearly a mile, ducking behind trees and nestling coyly in bushes. On the hill behind the site, a sign said 'CAFETERIA'. It did not look like the sort of place that would appreciate tents, or vice versa. I therefore hurtled on, with the sunset glittering on the water.

There is a current-operated ferry at Hampton Loade, connecting the two halves of a village of wooden bungalows. When I got there it was out of commission, its landing stages submerged in the flood. The river was howling down; just below the stage, in the lee of a tuft of grass, there was a tiny eddy. It could have been made for *Magdalen*. I tucked her in, tied her up, scrambled up the high bank and pitched the tent. After I had devoured boeuf bourguignon *en poche*, I moseyed off to the pub.

Not the least extraordinary feature of Scott's last expedition was the copious diaries kept by its members even during the final, fatal dash for the Pole. Keeping a diary is no joke if you have to write inside a sodden reindeer-skin sleeping bag in a temperature of $-30°$F, without light, after you have been dragging a thousand-pound sledge across crevasses all day. In fact keeping a diary is no joke even without these disadvantages. The writer must either sit cross-legged on the camp-bed, humping his back like a camel to keep it away from the slope of the tent's roof, or he must lie in the sleeping bag, resting the weight on one arm while he writes with the other. Either way, terrible aches soon set in, and the entries tend to become curt to the point of tediousness. My entry for 7 October, for instance, originally read, 'Got up. Went down river. Bed.' Fine while memory is fresh, but not calculated to excite the curiosity of Willie and Martin Llewellyn, who tell colourful stories like that all the time. Posterity could not be traduced; even at that evil-tempered hour, I knew I must do better.

It was therefore in search of a table to write at rather than strong drink that I repaired to the White Lion.

There were, as I had hoped, tables. Having sat down, I began to scribble away.

Much of the world's great literature seems to have been lashed up in taverns; take Doctor Johnson, Shakespeare and Dylan Thomas, to name but three. Matters seem to have changed fairly dramatically, however. The scritch-scratch of ball-point on exercise book nowadays seems to produce a nervousness in the average drinker. And after the silence come the questions.

These I answered with honesty. Breath was sharply drawn in and heads shaken. The man who collected the glasses was so moved that he showed me his torch, a chromium-plated one he had had since 1939. Then he told me about a chap who had gone across the ferry on just such a flood as this, and the wire had broken and they did not find him till weeks later. Nearly in Kiddyminster he was and smashed to pulp.

A man with tattoos, who seemed by his conversation to have been in something called the Merch, then joined in. His view was that there was a terrible draw to the weir at Holt Fleet. Not long ago a boatload of army blokes went over and their bodies was found miles downstream, horribly—

'Mangled?' I said, thinking back to the man by the Shrewsbury pike hole.

He looked at me with suspicion, as if wondering how I knew. 'How did you know?' he said.

'And the bridge,' said someone else, warming to the theme. 'Tell him about the bridge.'

'Ah.' The Merch man shook his head. 'Steel. There's steel under Arley Bridge.'

'Steel and a whirlpool,' said someone else.

I experienced a moment of quiet ecstasy. I was really in the Midlands now.

And sure enough, the talk swelled and flowed with tales of disaster, and then of human ingenuity baffled by superior cunning. I heard about a publican who had bet one of his customers twenty pounds that he could not drink sixty pints of beer in a day. After fifty-eight pints, the publican had refused to serve his man, on the grounds that he was drunk. A reverent hush fell. It was broken by another speaker who knew an old man who was due for a birthday, his eightieth. A party, with coach, had been arranged. But on the eve of the big day, some intelligent person checked the old man's birth certificate (a really Midlands thing to do) and discovered he had been having them on, and that he was only going to be seventy-nine! Well, of course they cancelled the party.

In a novel he would have died of mortification and disappointment. In the Midlands he is undoubtedly alive and hale and
plotting revenge.

The warnings of the doomsayers had a soothing effect, and I slept
deeply and at length. When I awoke, however, there was an
undertone of trepidation to the hearty thoughts with which I
greeted the day. What about the dreaded Eymore Rapids, for
instance? And, more immediately, was *Magdalen* still there?
Seized by a sudden panic, I rolled out of bed and lurched into the
weeping morning. *Magdalen* was there. I returned to the tent,
cursing myself for getting wet without first donning the oilskins,
dressed and packed.

Loading up was becoming second nature. Pump out the boat
(less water again this morning). Then lower the container down
the bank on a rope, and lay it crossways between the bow
half-deck and the thwart. After that the fish box, avoiding
spillage. Then the tent and camp-bed, wrapped in polythene and
wedged alongside the container. Last of all, the buckets – food,
camera and garbage, disposed around the feet. Loop the bow line
round a telegraph pole and abseil down the precipitous bank for
the last time. Insert rowlocks. Haul in mooring line, and push off
with an oar. The little whirlpools of the eddy suck at *Magdalen*'s
side. She seems to feel the thrill of life along her keel. A willow
tree goes past, its twigs jittering in the flood. The camping place
falls behind. Pulling into midstream, ship oars and extract Thermos. Eat breakfast: half a loaf of bread, a tin of corned beef, half a
jar of mustard and four chocolate biscuits. The river leaps and
sweeps from hole to hole, the swans keep well ahead, and mallard
whizz nervously into the drizzle. The banks are grey grass, grey
mud and grey trees in grey rain; *Magdalen* does ballroom dancing
in the eddies – the waltz and veleta, very stylish.

I was soon running into anglers, who greeted me cheerily,
telling me it would be harder work going back. I seemed to have
heard this joke before. By this time I was not really concentrating,
as the effort of digesting breakfast was drawing the blood away
from my optimism centres; the cowardice ganglia, meanwhile,

were ticking over nicely. The reason for this was the increasing nearness of the dreaded Eymore Rapids.

I had been told by the nice lady at the water authority that the main channel was to the left of centre, and that a mile below I was to take the channel to the left of the island, at which point there was a low waterfall. Below this, there was a line of rocks, shootable at its extreme right.

This was all very well, but it was raining and visibility was down to about twenty yards. By the time I heard the roar of mighty waters I was well stuck into elevenses and reclining at my ease on the life-jacket, And by the time I had woken up, I was halfway down phase 1 of the rapids. This is a mile of water full of lumps and brickbats, running in a noisy but picturesque manner between blackish precipices that I dimly discerned as densely wooded banks. Ideal life-jacket water; but water in which the navigator is well advised to stick to his oars. As all the world knows, it is far from easy to don a life-jacket while clinging limpet-like to a pair of seven-foot ash paddles. Halfway through deliberations aimed at finding a solution to this problem, a further roar announced the arrival of the low fall. Being somewhat preoccupied, I had my back to the low fall, and noticed it only as a line of tumbling water extending from one side to the other of the stream. So obese and corklike was *Magdalen* that she took it with scarcely a shudder. The line of stones flashed by—

And so much for the dreaded Eymore Rapids.

Once my heartbeat had returned to normal, I began to feel rather aggrieved. *Magdalen* bobbed along like a complacent cork. To look at her, you would never have known that ten days ago she had resembled a badly stacked pile of kindling. And of course she would not admit it, now. She was well aware that there would from now on be people to show off to, and she meant, in her dowager's style, to play up to them. She was not going to give me any chance to brag about how dangerous it all was. The mortifying thing was that there was very little I could do.

If you wanted a real thrill in *Magdalen*, the thing to do would be to choose a medium-sized waterfall, plunging, say, twenty feet into a cauldron of white water studded with basalt teeth, and take her over.

A word here in passing about one of the least publicized influences on the nation's travelling habits, viz. the human kidney. It is not known how many car crashes and air disasters have been produced, directly or indirectly, by the stress induced by fullness of bladder. Astronauts certainly show a fine freedom in these matters, as those whose task it is to clean out their suits have not hesitated to tell us; so presumably someone is spending vast sums on finding out.

Road and space travellers have it easy, however. Those who travel in small boats have bigger problems: they must take into account not only discretion, but balance. *Magdalen* was excellent in this respect, being virtually unrockable under the most urgent circumstances. I did, at the base of the Eymore, spare a rapid *requiescat* for the Canadian painter and wilderness hand Tom Thomson, who was drowned while canoeing in Algonquin Park in Northern Ontario. It is indeed a sad statistic, and a warning to us all, or anyway those of us who are male, that *ninety per cent of Canadian canoe fatalities are found, on recovery of the corpses, to have their flies unzipped.*

Below the dreaded Eymore, the traveller on water is in the presence of civilization; more than that, of one of the great mysteries.

The river runs slow and deep and smooth, seeming scarcely to crawl. The bankside trees drip second-hand rain into it, as if the sight of their reflections has reduced them to tears. Between the trees, crusted with green slime and a film of rain and rotting spores, are the landing stages; amazing confections of old railway sleepers and scaffolding poles, and rubber tyres and empty Domestos bottles, and lengths of lavatory chain and clothes line, all mingling in a remorseless downward slump, slow as a glacier, into the silt. Here and there, the first cabin cruisers of the river were going the same way at the moorings. And behind them, resting in the trees, are the bungalows.

The topmost part of this reach of the river is called Folly Point, and if this does not refer to the bungalows, it certainly should. After Spaghetti Junction and the Bull Ring, they represent the finest flowering of the Midlands imagination, lacking perhaps the money lavished on the fibreglass extravaganzas of Staines, but making up for this in conviction. In the gardens, platoons of gnomes fish, gambol, leap, sneer, sit and dig beside squadrons of flamingoes and New York blocks of vacuum-moulded sundials at the ends of miles of fibreglass colonnades. The structures themselves leer at the passer-by with rotting sash windows full of fly corpses. They sprout domes and minarets, cupolas and gazebos; architectural styles encompass Tara colonial in clap-board, Windsor Castle in roofing felt; seventeenth-century black-and-white under corrugated asbestos eaves, basic drive-in in flat galvanized sheeting; and – crowning achievement of a masterbrain – a chapter house in British Racing green corrugated iron. In summer, the verandas (the only thing they had in common were the verandas), must pullulate with bronzed humanity taking a few days away from the grind of commerce. In October, there was not a soul to be seen; only the drip of water from slimy beams and the half-heard tinkle of a voice, slurred with Babycham, reminiscing of Benidorm. It was uncanny to be the only human in the presence of this terrible beauty; shuddering, I passed on. But still, when ever I hear the drip of water or see a certain light on a muddy puddle, I am transported to that long, slow reach below the Eymore Rapids.

An hour later I was in a café in Bewdley, exchanging the coin of the region for two tins of hot Coke and a Mars bar. In the corner, a Space Invaders machine made its noises. Downstream lay a new world. Below Bewdley, the Severn becomes officially navigable.

Part Two

CHAPTER FOUR

Bewdley to Worcester

Bridgewater, Brindley, and the golden age – Bewdley sleeps – The cabin cruiser's graveyard – Stourport, and a collision – Health note – Our first lock – the uses of a bugle – The Alice Springs bargee – Encounter with a prophet – How to gatecrash a breakfast party – Franz Klammer goes fishing

The golden age of British waterways is generally reckoned to have begun in 1759, when the Duke of Bridgewater obtained an Act of Parliament giving him permission to construct a canal to link the coalmines on his estate with Manchester. The Duke was young and squashy-looking at the time; there is an engraving of him, posed limp-wristedly in front of his aqueduct and looking as if he could be knocked down with a wren's feather. His engineer, James Brindley, did the actual building. It is a reasonable bet that his Grace was putty in Brindley's hands, Brindley being a mill-wright of Scottish extraction who looks in his portraits as if he would have had no objection to taking his breakfast porridge frappé with barbed wire.

When Bridgewater's canal opened in 1761, it was immediately seen to be a good idea. It slashed to the bone the price of coal (previously carried or dragged over abominable roads by horses). It also materially assisted the development of the city of Manchester, which must have been thought to be a good idea at the time, however it may appear now. But most of all, it was brand new, and as such capable of being imitated.

The discovery that a chap could, by digging a ditch and filling it with water, not only become obscenely rich but also invent Manchester, had a galvanic effect on the British investor. Between 1761 and about 1840, when railway companies caught the public imagination, the country seethed with men bearing first theodolites, and subsequently shovels. Millions of words of fiction were written about thousands of miles of as yet undug waterway; investors queued up to invest their hard-won quids; and several canal companies actually built canals.

The Severn was to be one of the principal arteries of the new system, but the inhabitants of Bewdley were not taken in. Just as the Egyptians chose to ignore the invention of the wheel on the grounds that someone some day was going to get his toes badly squashed, the conservative spirit that inspires Bewdley to keep its Coca-Cola at blood heat suggested that if canals got built, someone some day would get his feet wet. In addition Bewdley had, since time immemorial, been the distribution point for goods coming up the Severn in trows from Bristol, because Bewdley men had fought for Edward IV at the battle of Tewkesbury, and had in consequence been exempted from ever paying river dues. What would happen to their nice trows and packhorse trains when the nasty canals came? Ruination, was what.

So when James Brindley asked them if he could join his new Staffordshire and Worcester Canal to the Severn at Bewdley, Bewdley said certainly not. Mr Brindley thus joined up his canal five miles downstream, at Stourport, and Bewdley said tch, tch, and sat on its hands. It is still sitting on them. The municipal arms features a nautical anchor. There is still a pub called the Pack-horse, and a fine stone quay downstream of the bridge. But there are no mooring rings on the quay; although Bewdley is shown as the limit of navigation on the waterway maps, the only boats I saw were tiny runabouts for hire.

Below the town, a cliff of red rock plunges into the water. At the base of the rock is a huge eddy, capable of spinning a seventy-foot boat in its own length. It is a dour and gloomy spot, and one where it would not be at all difficult to drown.

Magdalen signalled her disapproval by executing a double pirouette and attempting to jam her nose under a projecting ledge. A fisherman on the far bank watched without much interest as the oars leapt from the rowlocks and I crashed backwards into the container, unbalancing an open tin of sardines. We entered the reach below the rock stern first, engaged in profane speech, and oiled like Moroccan thieves. There had been other smells further up river; but they had lacked penetration compared to that of the sardines. I rowed hard, attempting to leave it behind, but to no avail.

An old man with a fishing rod frowned and said, 'You all right, son?'

'Oh yes,' I said. 'Certainly. It is only that there is no bath in view and I have got to live with myself for a long time and I am not smelling too good.'

'Ah,' said the old man, lifting his float from the water and scrutinizing his maggot. 'You ought to take up smoking.' I told him I had just given up. He shook his head. 'Kills the sense of smell,' he said. 'Very handy.'

The distance between us was growing now. He wrinkled his potato-like nose. 'Hello,' he said. 'Funny. I could be sure I smelt sardines, then.'

I smiled at him weakly, dug the oars into the water, and pulled smartly away. He was still sniffing suspiciously as he disappeared round the bend. Sweat poured off me as I tried to outdistance the reek, to no avail. So I washed everything with river water and sprinkled a bit of lemon juice about, and shortly *Magdalen* stopped smelling like a cannery and started smelling like a Mediterranean beach restaurant, which was at least slightly exotic.

Soon, I passed a noticeboard. It was facing downstream, so that it would be visible to boats heading upstream. It read:

BRITISH WATERWAYS BOARD
END OF SEVERN NAVIGATION

Between this notice and the sea, the Severn can be used by large boats. The waters I had travelled from its source might once have been an artery of commerce, but nowadays they are classified as fit only for fishermen and kayak artistes. The notice made *Magdalen* and me feel rather smug, like explorers strolling into the Red Lion in Anchorage, Alaska, and announcing that they had just come on foot from the North Pole.

The smugness soon gave way to amazement. For it is to the end of the Navigation that things come to die. Largest of these is

Bewdley, dreaming behind its unused quays. Smaller, but more numerous, are the cabin cruisers.

The heyday of cabin cruiser building seems to have been the early 1950s. At that time, boats were still made of wood, and styled as much like cars as possible. Once they must have been wondrous objects, full of fins and wings and bulging portholes, all gleaming with varnish and polished brass. Now they look less good; the first mile of the Severn Navigation has the air of the saloon bar of a public house close to a home for retired actors. Some of the hulks have been painted, but painted over the film of green algae that will be the undoing of the Folly Point bungalows. Some of them have been improved and extended. These would have been bought as bargains by the first-time boat owners, whose critical faculties were so numbed by the burgeoning spirit of Drake and Nelson that they ignored the battle zone where the wet rot from below met the dry rot from above.

The really gullible first-time owner is an astonishing specimen. Since his responses are similar to mine on first viewing *Magdalen*, I shall examine them in detail.

Having responded to the advertisement for '35-ft vintage runabout 200 H.P. Packard petrol engine needs attention lying Bewdley', he pockets the wife's nailfile in lieu of a bradawl and sets off for the riverside wearing a salty frown. On arrival he is greeted by a tired-looking individual dressed in soaking wet jeans, who waves a hand in the general direction of the mooring, tells him in a voice weakened by despair to go ahead and look, and makes an assignation for the snug bar of the Wobbly Elf in forty minutes' time. The first-time owner finds himself looking at thirty-five feet of diseased linoleum, moored by tight vertical bow and stern lines to overhanging willow branches. He steps aboard, grip slackening on the wife's nailfile. What he sees is a leaky wheelhouse from which rotting steps lead to (*i*) cabins, featuring bunks filled with empty bottles and old items of female underwear half-hidden under dense fronds of spirogyra and slime fungi, and (*ii*) the engine room, where the Packard mentioned in the advertisement crouches like an iron toad in a coil-deep gravy of river water and leaked oil. This is what his eyes see. What his brain registers – if you can call it a brain – is something else entirely, something which would leave Samuel Taylor Coleridge groping for adjectives after the second decanter of laudanum. The bunks are full of sensuous female bodies, rippling seductively in the June sunlight streaming through the gleaming brass port-holes. He rests his hands on a rust-pitted lump of metal in the engine room, muttering, 'What a flywheel!' (Actually, it's a magneto.) 'She'd clean up nicely,' he says, patting a spongy deck beam, the nailfile unheeded in his pocket. 'We'd do Brest the first year, just sort of pottering around. Then through the canals and across the Med. To Egypt, source of the Nile, down again to Suez – no trouble in this little beauty, shallow draught, made for the job – year after that Indonesia, then sort of hop up the Pacific to Panama, north-east route across Atlantic back to – erm – Bewdley. Piece of cake.' And he runs up the steps, by now wearing white ducks and a faultless yachting cap with an RYA badge, and writes out a cheque in the snug bar of the Wobbly Elf. Then he spends a year trying to patch up the bad bits with plywood and Mayo marble-pattern Formica, and finally unlooses the mooring ropes, at which point the whole works descends to the riverbed in a cloud of methane bubbles.

After this he buys a bicycle.

Cabin cruisers fall into three categories. There are the hazards to navigation, described above, which generally bear names inspired by the coronation of Her Majesty Queen Elizabeth II. Among these are *Sovereign Lady*, *Majestic Elizabeth*, and *Hieress [sic] of Light*. There are the cheeky chappies, less than twenty feet long, powered by outboard motors, and bearing names like *Diabola*, *Sweat Inspiration*, *Mik-Dor* or (two really splendid efforts) *Stimula* and *Fiesta*. Finally there are the gilded palaces of gin, bearing on their counters exotic ports of registration like Poole and Southampton, and on their pilot-house roofs radar scanners and VHF aerials. These were called expensive, thrusting names like *Avenger* and *Samantha IV*, and how they had got from their ports of registration to Bewdley is one of the eternal mysteries. Because while they could never have squeezed in to a canal lock, nor could they have arrived by sea, round Land's End and up the Severn. The salt would have melted them.

Magdalen appeared at this point to be feeling dignified scorn. Possibly she felt a bit there–but–for–fortunish about the hazards to navigation, because she stopped leaking. Certainly the obstreperous sleekness of the gilded palaces of gin discomfited her. In retaliation, she squatted lower in the water. Our speed dropped. The sardines wrapped us in a palpable cloud of vapour. But at this point, I refused to worry about the stink or the speed. For the fact that we were on the Navigation, and that the current had slowed to a crawl, meant that we were approaching a lock. So it was with a modest surge of adrenalin animating the heart muscle that we cruised past the notices saying PRIVATE – STOUR-PORT MOTOR YACHT AND BUNGALOW ASSOCIATION (I had never seen a motor bungalow before, and hope I never shall again) and into Stourport.

It was at Stourport that I had my first experience of the British canal system. I had tied up and gone ashore for a walk; the Stourport Basin, built by Brindley, has some fine eighteenth-century red-brick buildings. I paused to open a lock gate for a small boat, made of steel and about the same proportions as a well-chewed pencil stub. It contained a gentleman in leather trousers and two attractive Scottish ladies. Having bidden them farewell, I stood and admired the surface of the basin, encrusted with decaying hulks.

Then I heard the drone of an engine and saw a small cruiser of the cheeky chappie type, thickly festooned with fenders, hurtling across the water. Its skipper, a grey-faced person with a ragged moustache, was proceeding as if through a U-boat wolf pack, zag following zig fast enough to baffle a pilot fish. His crew, or wife as she may have preferred to be known, was crouched on the foredeck registering tension. He entered the lock obliquely; his crew leaped forward, dropping the rope and enabling him to smite the brick coping three times with the only parts of his hull not protected by fenders. She rushed to unwind the sluices, at which point he surged forward, ramming the gate. Owing to his frenzied revving of the engine, he was unable to hear the shouts from above; the gates opened and he moved in a debonair manner into the river, where the mooring rope trailing behind him wound itself lovingly round his propeller. As I withdrew, I heard him say to his wife, 'Well, it were better than last time.' If you see newspaper reports of *Cabin cruiser passes through lock – sixty injured*, you will know whom to blame.

By Stourport, civilization has taken a firm hold. Power stations creep down to the river, the banks are lined with concrete, and small boys peer at luminous fishing-floats under notices that say DANGER – NO TRESPASSING. The colour of the water had changed from black to grey-green with patches of iridescence; it had become slow.

We approached the first lock nervously. People on the bank told me, with what seemed indecent cheerfulness, that it was several miles downstream, well signposted and generally safe as milk. All very well for them, I thought; they live out their lives knowing only tiny sections of this great gleaming serpent. How could they judge the merciless power of it? It was entirely obvious that without an amazing display of skill and dexterity, not to mention sheer luck, *Magdalen* would be plucked into the weir stream like a lump of duck-fluff. I looked nervously over my shoulder.

A light drizzle was falling, hazing the horizon with grey. Along the banks, hazards to navigation swathed in leprous roofing-felt awaited transport to the mortuary. The sail with which I had covered the junk in the boat was soaked through; my waterproof garments, consisting of agricultural-weight plastic leggings and a Barbour jacket, had through some process unknown to science absorbed thirty or forty pounds of water, which expressed itself in drifts of steam emanating from collar and cuffs. My headgear, an excellent straw hat I bought for £1.25 in Ludlow when the man in the shop assured me that all Shropshire Lads wore them, felt as if Thor Heyerdahl had recently crossed the Atlantic in it. I was, in sum, extremely wet.

Health note. Those of a scientific bent may at this point wish to make an assessment of my mental and physical health at this, the beginning of the second major stage of the journey. If you are of squeamish disposition or if you hate to hear people whine, skip the next bit as far as the gap. All right, then. Are you sitting comfortably?

I was not. This was because of the bum nerve difficulty. Doctors know that there exists in the human bum a nerve which, when ground between the bum bone and a seat of unyielding elm, gives its owner gyp. This was now occurring, though the pain was tolerable provided one spent five minutes in every twenty standing on one leg and screaming with agony.

Also there was the hand problem. Well-meaning folk had told me before I started out that I was going to get blisters. Not so, fortunately. Instead, my hands, tiny, aristocratic, white and delicate, had started to grow. Since the bones had reached full size some years previously, the only sites for expansion were in the joints, which had with constant stretching become lengthy cylinders of cartilage. What they had gained in size they had, however, lost in flexibility; nine hours a day of tugging the recalcitrant blade had frozen them in an attitude resembling the claws of an arthritic condor.

Finally, something peculiar had happened to the colour of my skin. After my first night under canvas, I had become conscious that all might not be well, hue-wise. And as day followed day, an intensely disturbing truth began to come home: *I was turning blue.* It was an unfamiliar, but not altogether unpleasant sensation; once the initial shock had worn off it was possible to appreciate the clarity of the colour (half-way between Mediterranean-sky and Oxford) and the physical functions seemed in no wise impaired. Why was it happening? It had not bothered me before. But now, passing the crowded river banks of Stourport, people started to point and make remarks. It was time I found out.

Eventually the lock hove into view. It was on the northern side of a large island in the river. On the southern side was the weir, thundering dully in the drizzle. *Magdalen* crept timorously along the north bank. Far from showing an ambition to get whisked away by the weir stream, she seemed reluctant to move at all. Titanic gruntings and groanings at the oars produced a speed of one knot. Grasping a towline, I scaled a ladder set in the concrete and began dragging her towards the lock gates. She took this opportunity of demonstrating her wallow to port, a manoeuvre involving a sudden dart to the left and a sickening collision with the bank that she never failed to find diverting. When the echoes had died away I peered down into the depths. In her bilges, the puddle of dirty water, sardine oil and dying bankside vegetation did not seem any deeper than previously, which was a relief. But I would have to be careful. Just forward of the bow thwart, a belt of rot ran from the gunwale down the side, across the keel and up the other side to the other gunwale. A smart crack in the right place would bust her open like an egg, putting a serious cramp in the expedition's objectives. When I resumed towing, it was with great care, using a long line from well forward.

The lock-keeper watched our arrival from his glassed-in control hut. It was not, one presumes, an everyday occurrence during the month of October for a dripping bundle of rags to hobble by, cursing faintly, reeking of sardines and blue as a Touareg. But lock-keepers as a breed seem inured to surprise. This one opened his window and suggested that I hopped back into the boat. I mumbled something about the turbulence and he laughed cheerily and said, God bless you, there's none of that going *down*. So I proceeded in a gingerly manner down an apparently endless set of slimy rungs, alighting in the usual tangle of equipment, and sat, braced for the foaming rush of water that was going to splatter us all over the walls. I waited and waited; presumably the lock-keeper was toying with us, letting the fear do its work . . .

But the gates were opening. We were down. The whole experience had been about as turbulent as five minutes in a hospital lift. The lock-keeper waved, beaming through the drizzle, and said he'd ring the next lock down to tell it I was on my way. I pulled into the cut, which was perhaps a hundred yards long. Fat pike floats bobbed between clumps of reeds, watched by equally fat pike fishermen. There was no current here, away from the main stream of the river. *Magdalen* responded sluggishly to the oars; after a hundred yards my shoulders felt as if I had been carrying her, not rowing her. This was disturbing since I had to row *up* the Avon from Tewkesbury, and if she was practically unbudgeable in still water, it was anybody's bet how she would behave when battling against a river that was draining the Midlands after a fortnight of rain.

Meanwhile we were out of the cut and into the tail of the weir pool, and matters were once again proceeding with swiftness and vigour. A lash of whisky in the lunchtime coffee removed thoughts of upstream navigation; we moved on, singing hoarsely, through the rain down a flat and boring stretch of river infested with cross-looking anglers and devoid of anything interesting to look at, except a couple of 1950s public houses, which were closed. Another lock followed, opening briskly in response to a blast from the bugle.

A word here about the bugle. It was originally the property of my grandfather, who wrote about motor cars in the *Autocar*, in the days when people kept logbooks in which they recorded their journeys. He was among the first men to travel from London to Barcelona by motor-car, and wrote a book about it called, unsurprisingly, *The South-Bound Car*. In between diverting himself at Biarritz and getting stuck in a ford near Irun, he attempted to cause Pyrenean avalanches by blowing martial blasts on the bugle. The poor state of Spanish roads at the time (explicable to my grandfather by the fact that they were maintained by foreigners) is vividly borne out by the fact that the bugle's mouthpiece bears twin indentations that can only have been produced by a pair of upper incisors. It opened locks like magic. An unfortunate side-effect was the number of bird-watchers who wrote in to report trumpeter swans in new and fascinating habitats near Droitwich.

There is an old Chinese saying that whisky at luncheon leads to sloth in the late afternoon. While one cannot vouch for its accuracy in all cases it certainly seems to apply on the Severn immediately to the north of Worcester. Four p.m. accordingly found *Magdalen*'s power unit slumped over the oars and drifting aimlessly at perhaps half a knot in the centre of the stream. The drizzle had stopped, but a low grey sky still pressed down on the high grey water, and the world was a thick, wet place with me in the thickest wettest part of it. The willows on the banks trailed away to their distant grey vanishing points; nothing stirred except the reflections wobbling in the ripples from *Magdalen*'s bow as I shifted position in a futile attempt to stop my left leg going to sleep.

Then, in the distance, there came a light throbbing on the air. The throbbing grew louder, and a boat appeared round a distant curve and began to gain on us. I viewed it with some interest, as it was the first craft I had seen heading in my direction. I was sick of rowing; on this tedious stretch of water, anything was a diversion.

The thing turned out to be a narrow boat, seventy feet long and seven feet wide, of the type hired out to the general public. Its crew hailed me in a fluent Australian accent, and asked me if I required a tow. Replying that I did, I passed over the painter.

You may have noticed that when a tug wishes to haul a supertanker from A to B, it does not use a chain. Instead it uses a fat rope, or at the very least a hawser with a spring link in it. This is because a towed boat has a tendency to catch up with its tower, and then to drop back to the end of its line. If the line is rope, the towee bounces. If the line is chain, the towee has instantaneously to accelerate from its slow speed to the speed of the tower. This is a fascinating mathematical situation and has a choice of three results. Firstly, the tower may stop dead in the water until got under way again by the curses of its helmsman. Second, the towee may be yanked forward in a series of sharp jerks. And thirdly, the jerk may pull the stem right out of the towee.

Magdalen's painter was made of chain, so I could padlock her up safe from Midlands boat rustlers. Also, as you already know, the front portion of her hull was attached to the rest only by a mess of rotten kindling. The first jerk nearly put me overboard; the second produced a dreadful cracking noise from the forward planking; and the third had me windmilling on to the foredeck and groping for the after bollard of the narrow boat with a bit of old clothes-line.

After that, a conversation took place. It was pleasant enough, consisting of a bit of mutual back-slapping about the beauties of the Severn and a bit of polite incredulity about the fact that it was thought possible to row that thing (here *Magdalen* delivered herself of a dangerous shudder) to London. Unable to imagine why people from a nice sunny place like Australia would expose themselves to the arthritic rigours of the English autumn, I tried to find out whether they had chosen a narrow-boat holiday as a method of seeing lots of rain. (Back in Alice Springs in the fourth year of the drought: 'Cripes, Bruce, you're *still all wrinkly! Must have been reely wit!*') As we parted company from the narrow boat above the next lock, a metal-blue kingfisher swooped from an alder on the bank and raced into a hole in the clay.

'Cripes!' said the captain. 'A midget kookaburra!'

Next to the Camp House Inn at Grimley, just north of Worcester, there is a meadow where guinea fowl and peahens and bantams peck in the ruins of a huge frame tent. The landlord told me I could camp there, so I erected the tent with the door facing across a brown and turbulent pool to Bevere Weir. Beside the meadow were more bungalows.

I was reverently contemplating a roofing-felt replica of the South Fork Ranch buildings when I heard the discreet cough beside me. It proved to emanate from a small, stringy cove in gumboots, who worked (he said) for the British Waterways Board. We inspected *Magdalen* and the tent in a grave manner. He passed no comment about the holes, and nodded approvingly as I patched some of the worse rents in the tent with farmer's tape. Then he released upon me two pieces of information.

'You realize,' he said, 'that the Avon's closed.'

It took a while to sink in. When it did, the hair stood on end and beads of sweat began coursing around in all directions. 'Whaddayamean, closed?' I babbled.

'Shut,' he said. 'The lock's shut. For repairs. In Tewkesbury.' His small, weaselly eyes searched my face. 'You said you was going up to Warwick,' he said.

'I was.'

'Not by the Avon you wasn't,' he said. 'Canal goes over the Avon on a bloody great aqueduct. You'd never pull up that bugger. Even if you got across the bust lock. Which you wouldn't.'

'I—'

'What you oughter do,' said the wizened one, 'is take the Worcester and Birmingham Canal to King's Norton Junction, get the Stratford from there to Lapworth, and go down the Grand Union to Warwick.'

'Where?' I said. 'Tell me where.'

'Turn left at Worcester,' said Mr BWB. 'Then foller yer nose. There's a lot of locks, mind. The Tardebigge flight, the Lapworth flight, the Hatton—'

'Locks?' I said. 'No problem.' Euphoria shook me like a terriered rat. 'Can do. My speciality. Easy peasy, Japanesey, wash your face in Lemon Squeezy.' I have said some stupid things in my life, but that was the stupidest.

And that was the first bit of information.

'And talking of Lemon Squeezy,' said the stringy fellow, 'did you know you were bright blue? Matches your tent. Well, so long,' he said, lurching off into the dusk.

I looked at the fly-sheet. I looked at myself. We were indeed the same colour. It was a cheap fly-sheet, bought especially for the trip. I pressed it with my hand. The hand came away bluer. Diagnosis!

And that was the second bit of information.

The Camp House Inn sounds as if it ought to be a gay bar, but it's not. Someone told me that it was part of a Roman camp, once. The landlord, a very jolly man whose cheerful children trooped into the bar to be said good night to, said rubbish. Someone built a tower here to watch the ford across the Severn, was all.

Gradually the place filled with Midlands moustaches and their offspring. The offspring bummed 10 p's from their parents for the juke box. One girl, whose father wore a drape coat, ten-inch drains and a Tony Curtis, had the mixture dead right; two Jam tracks, then an Elvis for the old man, repeat the mixture *ad lib.*

I sat in the corner and worked out a new route. An old man sidled up to me and told me of the glories of Worcester. He said there was a place near the cathedral with a vast bow window on the first floor, from which you could see the world spread out at your feet and people on the towpath walking like liddle dolls. He said that in his view it was the best breakfasting spot in the world and that it was called the Diocesan Club. Members only, and full of tough old women with white hair, he said, but he betted nobody would have the nerve to ask who I was, so why didn't I just tie up the liddle boat under the cathedral and nip up for some eggs and bacon? I failed to get the address of this oasis as I was being distracted by a man with eyes as innocent as a baby's, who was very drunk. He was telling a water bailiff, whom he seemed to have recently met for the first time, that he was going to be perf'ly frang with him, and tell him from the bo'm of his heart as he loved his mum so help him forgo'n wha' he was goin' say.

On the map, the blue line of the Worcester and Birmingham Canal was hatched with the arrowheads of locks. There were tunnels, too. It all sounded very exciting. To the south of the canal were the villages of Upton Snodsbury, close to North Piddle,

Flyford Flavell, Libbery, and Rous Lench. Verily, I mumbled in a wash of ale-borne sentiment, this is the Heart of England.

Later that night, I lay on the camp-bed contemplating the locks stretching uphill to Birmingham and feeling, fool that I was, positively relieved that the Avon was closed. Outside I heard distant footsteps blundering, and the squawks of trampled peahens. The footsteps stopped. In their place there started a unmistakable sound.

'Hughie!' a voice cried. 'Huuuuggghhiieee!'

I mean, how Midlands could you *get*?

Early the next morning boots started sloshing around outside. Crawling into the half-light. I was rewarded by the sight of a dozen fishermen, baskets on backs, wandering round in circles in the meadow. They cannot have been the first, as the grass had disappeared, churned to chocolatey mud. Withdrawing into the tent and lighting the stove, I drank some coffee and began to roll up the sleeping bags. There was a crash, a long-drawn out howl, and the sound of fierce but muffled Midlands swearing.

The Severn is notorious for its high banks. The traveller who wishes to climb from river to dry land does so at the peril of his life, unless he uses crampons. The meadow in which I was camped was reached by a near-vertical gully of greasy slime, on which were a few decoy steps. Examination of the steps the previous night had shown them to be rotten to the core, so I had avoided them.

Not so the fisherman, who had landed full-toss in *Magdalen*'s bottom. Nor, indeed, his mate. The mate was a small man, with the usual high Midlands power-to-height ratio. He was proceeding at a handy four miles an hour. On his back he had a heavy wicker basket and rod holdall, so it is unlikely that he could have changed course even if he had wanted to. His booted foot descended on the first step. The step gave way. His jaw and eyebrows flew in opposite directions, the moustache remaining static. His feet flew up until his body assumed the 9.15 position. Gravity seized him. The howl started, receded and ended. Franz Klammer could not have done it better.

I picked them up, hosed them off, and lent them a rope to get up the bank and to their fishing pegs. They did not seem tremendously grateful; perhaps they thought it was all my fault. It is always hard to tell what, if anything, fishermen are thinking. Particularly in the Midlands.

An hour later, the boat was packed. A thin skin of mist lay over the river, hiding the turbulence of the weir stream. The first fishermen were half asleep as I pulled past them. Two hours later, I was in Worcester.

CHAPTER FIVE

Worcester to Tardebigge

*The march of civilization – I get excited about locks – Magdalen
irritated by canals – The Worcester Commandery – Small boys on the
towpath – A boating lesson – The vigilante who saved Brum – Autumn
on the canals – The long and winding road – My morning routine –
Singing hymns to the ungodly – How to build a canal – How to get
through a tunnel – How to get horribly mangled – I begin to hate locks –
The curse of the Midlands*

By Worcester the Severn has become urban and proud of it. It is lined with large boathouses, from which competitive rowing takes place. The banks are concreted, and sprinkled with fishermen, broken glass and enthusiastic notices about football teams, done in spray paint. The river, has, one feels, grown up. It is hard to think of it as the toddler falling down the rocky sides of Plynlimmon, or even as the adolescent burning it up in the Severn Gorge. It is corseted by weirs, regulated by locks and surrounded by the results of its own prosperity. The traveller in a small and scruffy boat feels somewhat out of place.

Until, that is, he notices the bridge. The centre arch, where the channel passes, bears at its highest point many friction stripes from fibreglass upperworks. It was encouraging, now that the river had gone all professional, to think of rum-mad gin palace proprietors belligerently hurtling their twenty-foot superstructures at eighteen-foot headrooms.

Below Worcester Cathedral, the left bank of the river becomes a high brick wall. Suddenly there appears in the wall an oblique cut, ending in a pair of narrow wooden gates. Across the gates was written DIGLIS BASIN. Diglis Basin marks the bottom end of the Worcester and Birmingham Canal. It was here that I met my first still-water lock-keeper.

I had been told the previous night that the locks joining the Diglis Basin to the Severn were keeper-operated. But in the keeper's cottage I was told by a small, glinting-eyed man that I could operate them myself, if I liked.

Gosh, I said, can I really? Thanks a *lot*.

He gave me a curious look, as if he thought I was taking the

[87]

mick, and asked if I had a windlass, because you needed a windlass to get through locks. I replied that I did not have one but was looking forward to getting one, and he pointed at a chandlery where one could be bought, and said he supposed I hadn't done much travelling on the canals before and where had I come from and what in? And when I told him he sat down pretty quickly in a British Waterways Board chair and started shaking his head. I left him to it.

They sounded fairly amazed in the chandlery, too. Someone broached the subject of tunnels. The Worcester and Birmingham Canal, they said, was liberally provided with these. Unpowered craft were not allowed to go through them. Anyway they were horrible places, dark and wet and generally very dangerous. Seeming to detect negative thinking, I tried the light laugh and said that I would probably be able to struggle through somehow, even if it meant getting a tow.

They said yes, it was possible I would get a tow, but . . . well, there weren't many boats on the canal this particular week, it being between the end of the summer season and the half-term rush . . . well, it would be nice and peaceful, and they supposed that there was a sort of vague chance. So back I zipped to do the lock, meditating on the pessimism of canal folk and swinging my shiny new windlass. (A windlass is a winding handle for use on the kind of lock you have to operate yourself.)

After I had gone through the first lock, I was beginning to see that there might be a basis to the gloom. After the second, I was just about sure. But it was too early to make firm judgements; after all, any tedious and repetitious task was difficult to begin with. One had to wait until one had evolved a system, and then one flew past obstacles without noticing them. Or so I thought, fool that I was.

Magdalen felt different in still water. Solider, steadier. A lot harder to row.

The canal seemed very narrow after the river. On either side of the ribbon of dirty water, industrial buildings rose like cliffs full of windows. Wastepipes jutted threateningly from factories: there was no sound but the lick of ripples against the hull and the distant boom of Worcester's legendary one-way system.

I had a vague idea that the day's cultural visit could be to the Royal Worcester procelain factory. One of the few British works which can trace their descent directly to the years when porcelain was as magical a substance as cast iron to the builders of Ironbridge, and when its makers were regarded with the same awe as alchemists (which they sometimes were, on the side). But nowadays, the Royal Worcester factory presents to the canal many steel-framed windows through which can be seen huge stacks of unglazed lavatory bowls. On the pane of one of these windows, someone had stuck a notice saying IF YOU HAD SEX LAST NIGHT, SMILE. *Magdalen*, already humiliated by coming up two locks full of orange peel and other scum, and further battered by a sweaty pull through motionless and filthy water, did not find this at all amusing. Instead of visiting the place, both of us frowned with great severity, and passed.

Soon after this, the canal dived under a bridge, narrowing as it went and ending in a high wooden wall on which was growing an attractive selection of dandelions, brambles and even a pygmy lilac bush. This was disconcerting, and somewhat disheartening. Could it be that the canal had closed down without anybody realizing? Certainly there was very little traffic. None, in fact. Perhaps the lock-keeper had been humouring me, thinking our conversation was an elaborate joke . . . But the map said the canal continued, so I got out and reconnoitred on foot. And sure enough, the wooden wall was a lock gate.

The gate of my first narrow lock! It was a moment tremulous with romance. We went up it; and at the top, behind a quay set with attractive tea tables, was the Commandery.

The Commandery is a building begun, like most of the best buildings, shortly after the Norman Conquest, and still under construction. It owes its name, redolent of Malta, Cyprus, and warrior monks, to the fact that rumour connects it with the Knights Hospitaller, a military order dedicated to the patching up of those unzipped by enemy action during the Crusades. It was a hospital between the eleventh and sixteenth centuries. During the Civil War, the closing phases of the Battle of Worcester took place in its grounds. It is now a museum. In one of its rooms, formerly used for the comfort of those awaiting death, there is a fresco of the disembowelling of St Erasmus. St Erasmus is the patron saint of stomach-ache, and after a look at the painting one can see why. In the next-door room was an exhibition of chain saws.

In the grounds of the Commandery there is a fragrance garden. The man sitting at the ticket desk in the magnificently timbered great hall pointed out that just over the wall from the fragrance garden is the busiest fish-and-chip shop in Worcester, and returned to his *Private Eye*.

The Midlands, it seemed, was a place of exciting contrasts.

The canal in Worcester is a small boys' heaven. A lot of them sit and fish, with the look of introspective superiority common to anglers everywhere. Others roar up and down the towpaths on bicycles, pausing for altercations with the fisherfolk about who is in whose way. A third group, the progressives, crouches under a bridge away from the parental eye, and surveys the passing scene through dense clouds of cigarette smoke.

The fishermen are hard to talk to. The obvious opening is to ask them if they have caught anything, to which they immediately reply, 'A couple of little 'uns,' and return to the contemplation of their floats. The bicyclists are going too fast. The progressives, however, had nothing to do but talk. One of them turned down his tape machine, eyed the boat and ground his No. 6 underfoot. Then he said, 'What are you doing?'

I told him. There was a pause. Then he said, 'Livin' rough, are you?'

'I suppose so.'

'Where are you goin'?'

'London.'

Another pause. Was this the old zingola? Dignity was at stake. But after a quick reappraisal of the filthy boat, the appalling straw hat and the blue skin, he seemed reassured. 'What for?' he said.

'Fun. Doesn't it look like fun?'

A pause. Finally, 'Yeah. Got any fags?'

So much for the progressive element.

Finally I fell into conversation with Ian and Oliver, two extremely nice twelve-year-olds who, if they fitted into any category, fitted the cyclists; they were, however, serious thinkers on the lookout for anything that combined information with diversion. They proved their basic good nature by pedalling ahead and getting the locks ready, reducing transit time from ten minutes to five and probably rupturing themselves in the process. With their assistance, the grimmer portions of Worcester flowed swiftly by. We made courteous farewells in the outer suburbs, and they accepted my gifts of chocolate with dignified reluctance.

As Saturday afternoon became Saturday evening and Worcester turned into a series of playing fields and industrial estates, the crowd changed. Now the walkers were older. There was one heavy-set girl with a haircut like a black pudding-bowl who was on her way to visit her sister in some outer suburb. She let slip the information that she had never been in a boat before. There was not a ripple on the canal, and there had been no traffic all afternoon. It seemed like a golden opportunity; I got out, she got in, and I dragged her for a full ten yards before she got up, fell over, tried to save herself with one hand, and plunged in, throwing up a great fan of water. I rushed back, hoping she would come to the surface at least once, so I could get a grip on her. How I would get her up the bank I did not know, but I was prepared to try, because I did not wish to have a drowning on my conscience.

Actually she seemed to swim rather well, lying flat on her stomach and kicking with a will, crying 'Yoop! Yoop!' the while. I extended a hand from the bank. She ignored it, and rose like Venus from the water, drawing herself to her full height and dripping, apparently standing miraculously on the surface. Amazement robbed me of speech. Then I realized that the edge of the canal was only a foot deep.

'I'm *so* sorry,' I said. 'Can't think—'

'It was my fault,' she said heavily. 'I'm trying on a new dress at me sister's.'

'That's just as well,' I said.

'It was my fault,' she said again, and climbed through the hedge. The last I saw of her she was plodding across a disused quarry, dripping but by no means discomposed.

Ten minutes later, around the bend in the cut, the whizz and splat of air gun pellets sounded like a small discreet war. I bellowed that I was coming, rounded the bend, and came upon the Vigilantes – three spotty fifteen-year-olds with air rifles. They had shot several tin cans, presumably because they had run out of rats, moorhens and kingfishers. (The only wild life within a ten-mile radius of Worcester seems to be the fishermen.) They were a cheery, lethal bunch. The cheeriest and most lethal said he had recently moved from Brum. There he claimed to have infiltrated the underground city, apparently an exact replica of the overground city, that Brum holds prepared against nuclear war. There are roads and shops and everything down there, he said. The entrances are next to the entrances to the shops. You know that door next to the door of Woolworth's? Well, that's the entrance to the underground Woolies. It works like that, sort of, see?

He was okay, though. He had his .22 air rifle.

See that missile? ZINGGGGG!

After the Tolladine locks on Worcester's north-western out-skirts, there is a long pound. (A pound is what canal folk call a stretch of canal without locks.) After the M5 motorway there are few buildings; green fields once again roll down to the waterside, and farmhouses crouch behind coppices. There was rumoured to be a public house at Dunhampstead which was a *grand rendezvous des canalistes*, so I pressed on as the light faded. But it soon became apparent that I had misjudged things; nightfall was going to leave *Magdalen* and her power unit well short of the oasis.

Summer had finally decided to turn into autumn. The trees had a sprinkling of yellow leaves, and oaks bombarded the canal with acorns. In the water, the weeds were blackening and starting to rot; the air of early evening had a hard, damp chill to it, and the breath of winter filtered across the months.

The canal stretched ahead, a ribbon of looking-glass fringed with dying reeds. The sun rolled towards the horizon; every mile or so, the disappearing light outlined a humped bridge whose reflection completed an oblate O in the water. *Magdalen* pushed firmly on at a rate of about forty oarstrokes to the minute. After a time, a sort of glaze settled over the world; the auto-pilot cut in, and the rowing became a soothing, rhythmic process. Soon I seemed to be flying above the loaded boat and the long, converging strip of the canal, watching the sprawl of Worcester and the shadows of trees and church towers stretch with the falling sun; while ahead to the east, where the shadows lay thickest, the hills gathered and the beams of lock gates shone white in the dusk. And even beyond that a red glow hung in the sky; sodium glare lights strung like necklaces of grubby amber along the streets of Birmingham.

Night, to sum up, was falling.

There now appeared on the left bank a green field running up to a thirty-foot cliff of red earth, down which the roots of two colossal oak trees snaked. The field itself was dotted with shaggy ink-cap mushrooms, luminous white in the final rays of the sun. Tying *Magdalen* to a tent peg slammed into the bank, I set off to ask permission to camp.

The farmhouse was huge, made of red brick. Behind it was a yard with barns, implement sheds, stables and pens full of shadow. A sheepdog, tied in a shed, made no sound. It did not even look particularly interested. The yard was empty, except for the shadows. The bell rang tinnily in an empty room. No-one came. But there was a light on, so I walked round the house and found another door, facing into the garden. This time an elderly man answered. He looked more like a schoolmaster than a farmer. Through the window I could see an old woman with her feet up in front of a brass fender. The man told me that I could certainly camp in his field, if it was his field. He gave the impression that he did not quite know which of the fields belonged to him.

So I left them in their odd house surrounded by silent pens full of shadows, and put up the tent and ate ink-caps and boeuf bourguignon and boiled rice. Outside, the owls shrieked. It was a lovely place, and might have been on another planet. I occupied

[93]

myself by trying to remember what my children looked like. It seemed unduly difficult. When I went to sleep the chill of the night fog pierced tent and sleeping bag, and I had uneasy dreams.

One of the major luxuries of life on the waterways was that the early morning cup of coffee could be manufactured without stirring from the warm depths of the sleeping bag. Accordingly I drowsed, while the tent filled with steam and a female announcer wittered soothingly about Haydn on Radio 3.

To make morning coffee: take 2 oz Nescafé, 3 oz sugar (white – no cranks) and half a tin of condensed milk. Place in large jam-jar (the cup had fallen overboard the previous day, in a more than usually fetid lock) and mix with boiling water to as thin a paste as possible, given the limited space available. Blow on the resulting sludge until cool enough to drink.

Take a sip. SHAZAM!

The spine, still wallowing about on the camp-bed, suddenly stiffens with a rattle of vertebrae. The heartbeat, previously a lolloping fifty-five to the minute, accelerates to 140. The eyes start from the head, and the brain, which has hitherto been wondering whether that rather nice-sounding young lady on the radio had any idea that she was in what must be the smallest and rankest bedroom in the British Isles, leaps into forward motion with a clash of gears. ACTION!

Hurling myself out of bed, I pull on three jerseys, corduroy trousers and gumboots. Books and navigational equipment (maps) are slapped into Tupperware boxes and shoved into the container. Sleeping bags are wrung out, forced into polythene bags, and crammed on top of the maps and books. The whole is then rendered rattleproof with anything that is left lying about and is not actually squirting water, such as old socks, the clean clothes I would have put on last night if I had had the willpower to take off my existing clothes, and the washing and shaving bag, unopened for the same reasons. The lid is then screwed on to the container with the palms of the hands, to avoid finger damage. After the container was finished, the fish box was filled with its usual load of water-resistant gear.

At this point in the striking camp procedure, it was necessary to go outside. This was a process akin to leaping fully clothed into an iced bath; the sun was usually levering itself up through some trees somewhere, but more often than not it had chosen to do so behind thick blankets of cloud, which would be producing something pretty bracing in the driving rain line. Into this the camper crawls, shuddering, and sets about his tasks.

The groundsheets are folded, and the tent and fly-sheet pegs plucked from the dew or, more usually, hoarfrost. After the fly-sheet has been folded and more blueness transferred to face and hands, the tent is chased across the meadows, released from the thorn bush in which it has come to rest, and sworn at for a brief interval. The camp-bed is then hauled asunder and swathed in plastic. Various buckets are filled with rubbish, binoculars, and anything else that is lying about.

That's it.

On the Severn, the whole works then had to be transported down a ten-foot bank, with the aid of ropes and, on particularly weak mornings, pulleys. The great (some would say only) joy of the Worcester and Birmingham Canal was that the banks were in many cases only six inches high. An even greater joy on this particular morning was that *Magdalen*, whose standard overnight leaking left a foot of water in her bottom, was dry as a bone. She had finally swollen up!

Loading commenced to the accompaniment of fortissimo selections from *Hymns Ancient and Modern*, the revised version. The welkin was ringing to a new version of 'Lead Kindly Light', viz:

I have a pocket torch because it is past lighting-up time;
With it I can see where I am going.

when I became aware that I was being watched. On the far bank four men in waterproof clothing were standing with their mouths open. It seemed only civil to bid them good morning.

The canal was filling the bottom of the valley with mist, in which we were all standing up to our knees. Perhaps it looked as if I was heaving my tent into the water, and they thought I was a loony and that was why they weren't answering.

'Lovely day,' I said.

Turning their backs as one man, they began talking among themselves. Possibly they were fishermen. But even fishermen were not as boorish as *that*. Their conversation drifted across the canal; eavesdropping revealed the truth. They were indeed fishermen. More, they were the committee of a fishing club, organizing a competition. It was hardly surprising that they would not speak to mere mortals.

For some reason, when I embarked that day I made a terrible noise and disturbance in the water, frightening many fish in the process. It was probably exhaustion.

Since canals are flat and Britain is not, the builders of canals were forced to take measures to stop all the water gurgling into the sea. There are two basic methods of doing this. The earliest, popularized by Brindley, is to keep the whole thing on one level by building cuttings, embankments and aqueducts. When a range of hills interposes between you and your destination, you follow the contour line round the side. The later method, which makes canals shorter but more expensive to build, is to run your canal in a more or less straight line, obliterating large obstacles by building ladders of locks and smaller ones by drilling holes through them. These holes are known as tunnels, and since my interview in the chandlery the idea of them had been gnawing somewhat at the back of my mind. Not that I was *frightened*, mind you. It was just that the chandlery view of a tunnel conjured up the lair of a frightful lugworm, streaming water from roof and walls, thick with mysterious gases, and probably haunted by the drunken ghosts of bargees. Thus it was with an absolute minimum of good cheer that I pulled past the public house at Dunhampstead (a mere 400 yards up the canal from where I had stopped: a brilliant move and one typical of the sense of timing that had characterized my voyage to date) and on through the gradually lightening morning.

Shortly after Dunhampstead the canal bends slightly to the right, the banks grow higher, and the waterway disappears into a nasty black arch in the side of a hill. Here I rested on my oars, pondering. *Magdalen* responded more vigorously with a wallow to port, swerving abruptly to the left and ramming the bank. I picked myself up from the bottom and ate a hearty breakfast of cream crackers, Golf biscuits, salmon paste and French mustard. Then I took stock of the situation.

The far end of the tunnel was visible. It was about half the size of the entrance. The tunnel itself was sixteen feet wide, which gave me a foot's clearance each side of my oars. The chandlery had given me a bit of paper that said it was illegal to go through it without a life-jacket, horn, whistle, accomplice, week's supply of cheese sandwiches and experienced Canoe Führer. Faugh, I said, turning briskly in mid-canal. Let them eat cake. And in we went.

I would like to say right away that it is by no means easy to direct a rowing boat through the bowels of the earth with only a foot's clearance for your oars. After a hundred yards or so you lose your bearings and begin to imagine you are suspended in orbit round one of the dark planets of Alpha Centauri. You also imagine you are going sideways, so you pull extra hard with your right oar and are surprised to collide with the left-hand wall of the tunnel. You then attempt to push off, but the hydrodynamic characteristics of a badly patched rowing boat give it the inertia of an aircraft carrier, and after five minutes' feeble splashing you are delicately poised *across* the tunnel. At this point it occurs to you that if anything else was to come through, like for instance a seventy-foot narrow boat staffed by Midlands drunks, you would probably be in their way, not to say drowned and horribly mangled. So you give a violent hoick with the right oar again, and rediscover that while this move certainly turns the boat, it also drives it forward. You hit the wall again, and start to feel a strong urge to blubber. Repressing this with an effort of will, you flail at the walls with the spare paddle until you are once again in the approved shell-in-gunbarrel position.

But after your dervish-like whirlings you can't remember which way you were heading before all the trouble started. So you row on anyway, using only the tips of the oars, hearing imaginary narrow-boat engines and watching your life to date flash past in glorious Technicolour. If you keep ten per cent of the resolutions you make on the way out of a BWB tunnel, beatification will be yours, no sweat. Finally you arrive in the blessed daylight, and are able to take stock of your surroundings before you either proceed towards your destination or, having become disorientated and returned to your original entrance, start all over again.

I had a third option thrust upon me. While I was still twenty yards inside the tunnel I heard a whirring noise. When I looked around, a huge bow, painted with bright diamonds of red and yellow, was gleaming in the sunlight beyond the tunnel mouth. Digging in the oar blades, I hauled them through the water. The whirring grew louder, and the water began to shrink down the tunnel walls, sucked from in front of the great bow wave under the narrow boat's nose. The roof of the tunnel passed above me; *Magdalen* started to rise on the wave; I gave one last pull and crashed into the first bramble bush in the daylight. A man with a cloth cap and an open mouth stared horror-struck from the tiller of his brilliantly painted craft as it fed itself into the black hole in the hillside. I lay and listened to my heart slow down, watching two more working boats, painted like rainbows, cargo spaces empty, noses hooked and guarded with taut little tents of green tarpaulin, follow the first into the tunnel, *Magdalen* rocked in their wake, almost as if she was testing herself to see if she was still there, I knew how she felt. Five minutes longer in the tunnel and we would have been . . . well, horribly mangled.

If you really want to upset a canal freak, you go up to him or her and say, 'I have done the thirty and six in two hours, fifty minutes.' He or she will turn pale and probably call you a liar.

They took me eight hours.

The thirty and six are locks: six above Stoke, a spot near Droitwich where brine is pumped out of the ground; and immediately after them, thirty leading up to Tardebigge top lock, the start of a nine-mile pound that leads into central Birmingham. The thirty and six are one of the wonders of the waterway system, on a par with the twenty-nine Devizes locks on the Kennet and Avon Canal. (The Devizes locks were allowed to fall into disrepair, no doubt by sensible folk who had had to work the ruddy things; they are now being restored. While this is probably laudable, there is a reasonable case for saying that by the same token rowing galleys, with their merry laughing slave crews, are also ripe for restoration. In fact there is probably a Heritage masochist somewhere who has already done it. When I finally purchase my Heritage home, the electric lights, pintables and Asteroids machines will work off a huge treadmill. And I bet the coach parties who swarm through my box office will pay to have a go on it, too. Bitter, you may say. All I can tell you is that the Tardebigge locks breed bitterness.)

I arrived at the locks shortly after lunch, having spent an enjoyable late morning being chased by man-eating Alsatians across industrial estates. As a gesture of reprisal, a huge sardine-oil slick was left covering the canal.

Soon after the oil slick a small boy rushed out on to the towpath and asked for a ride. He couldn't swim, so I said no, and he began hurling stones with inspired inaccuracy. Then he shinned up a tree and gibbered at me like a monkey. I exchanged superior glances with an eleven-year-old girl and continued on my way deeply mortified.

A narrow lock is a form of civil engineering that enables boats to travel up and down hills. Typically, it resembles an open grave containing water and, by the smell of it, corpses. The usual dimension is seven feet wide and seventy-two feet long. It has double gates at the downhill end and a single gate at the uphill end – don't ask me why. It is filled and emptied by means of hand-cranked sluices known as paddles. On arriving at the lock, you open the bottom gates, tow in the boat, shut the gates, and fill it up with water by opening the top sluices, sorry, paddles, with your windlass. The boat rises. When the lock is full, you open the top gate, tow the boat out, and close the gate. You are then free to go, having risen about seven feet. The process has occupied a mere ten minutes of your time.

Thirty-six locks occupy three hundred and sixty minutes of your time. My calculations indicate that opening the sluices requires about fifty pounds' pressure each. The gates demand a similar effort from the legs. A few simple equations therefore show that working up the Tardebigge locks is equivalent to carrying just over five and a half tons 250 feet uphill in six hours, not counting the weight of the boat. This is what is known in the snug bar at the House of Lords as a bit of a shag.

It was Sunday afternoon, and many charming people were taking their post-closing-time constitutional on the banks. It would have been pleasant to linger and chat of this and that, but the strollers rather naturally shied away from the shambling blue ruin, clad in plastic trousers, filthy shirt, blood, sweat and a four-day beard, dragging its boat in and out of the locks. The shambling ruin was itself seeing matters through a glass darkly, since the unaccustomed effort of rowing in still water was taking its toll even before the staircase locks started.

There were those who took pity. A thirteen-year-old girl called Tracy hopped into the boat and insisted on going up the lock, watched by her awestruck brother and sister. The brother, who was the youngest and had the look of one of life's victims, said it was okay, she had got her swimming gold. He explained that to get the swimming gold you had to swim thirty-three lengths of the school pool in your pyjamas. I was on the point of demanding that she change into her pyjamas in order to ensure correct flotation when I noticed that she had discovered the wellspring of gastronomic delights, viz. the tin containing the chocolate biscuits. They left me a few locks later, having been a great help. The last I heard of them, they were telling the brother that he had to muck out the horse before tea. When he said he never rode the horse and indeed hated riding the horse, they told him that he was revealing his ignorance of the concept of sharing, under which some rode while others scraped dung off stable floors. My heart ached for the poor devil. I advised him to defy them, and we parted.

Future sufferers at Tardebigge may be interested to know that the best helpers are unquestionably those under fifteen. The elderly wish to talk, but are too infirm for the harsh business of applied hydraulics; while men between school-leaving and retirement age tend to be having a well-earned rest from the labours of the week. Their wives are usually pretty and a bit drunk, having spent lunchtime in the pub, so they are ripe for a bit of conversation, but disinclined to help. The menfolk are even less obliging, partly because the Midlands Sunday luncheon is a serious business demanding the dark suit, and partly because they are not unnaturally suspicious of this filth-encrusted semi-human who is not only rowing to London (wherever that may be), but also quite transparently chatting up the missus.

There are, in total, fifty-eight locks on the Worcester and Birmingham Canal. The numbers are written on the beams, to assist those navigators who have left their sextants in their other suits. By the time I was at number forty-seven, eleven from Tardebigge top lock, it was pitch dark, I was shattered, and *Magdalen* had lost two square feet of paint.

It was at this point that the Midlands, which I had been cursing with some freedom on the Tardebigge flight, began to exact a terrible retribution.

CHAPTER SIX

Tardebigge to Lapworth

The camp at lock forty-seven – Methane and rats – A Midlands welcome – Climate by Wagner, scenery by Garcia Marquez – The Wast Hill tunnel – An inner dialogue – Terror, grins, and whippets – Fishing with malice aforethought – The Wast Hill tunnel again – The white zone of the Stratford Canal – A sentimental butcher – Rain – Attempted murder, British Waterways style – More rain – The Lapworth flight – Shula Archer and Mateus Rosé

Immediately below lock forty-seven of the Tardebigge flight there is a small, stagnant pond. On the side opposite the towpath, reeds and small elder trees are invading the mud. Just above the mud is a tiny patch of rank grass and thistles terminating in a barbed-wire fence. Over the barbed-wire fence is a vast field of grass.

Night was falling as I arrived at lock forty-seven, and as usual I had left pitching the tent till far too late. The large grass field looked extremely inviting, and had the added advantage of being out of sight of any habitation, which meant that no farmer was likely to raise an objection, which in turn meant no traipsing about the countryside asking permission. It was therefore irritating to find that the grass field had recently been manured by one of those large machines that works on the helicopter in the latrine principle.

For one who has done forty-seven locks of the Worcester and Birmingham, however, lumps of dung hold few terrors. It was the work of a moment to clear a tent-sized area with a few blows of the gumboot, and begin erecting the shelter. What humane farmer would put cattle to graze on a recently manured field? (Cattle, as you undoubtedly know, are single-mindly dedicated to trampling both tents and their occupants down to ground level.) Yes indeed, every cloud has a silver lining, I thought, booting aside the final lump and busying myself with hammer and tent pegs.

But of course I was in the Midlands, and should have known better. There are no silver linings on the Worcester and Birmingham. As the tent blossomed on its poles, there was a noise of mass blundering and sixty Charolais cattle appeared over a rise in the

[103]

ground, filled with idiot curiosity. Charolais resemble centurion tanks with thick coats of white hair. Having once witnessed a half-grown Charolais bullock kick its proprietor through a closed stable door, I beat a hasty retreat, pitching the tent beside the canal on a bed of thistles, some (but not all) of which I was able to lacerate with my cutlass. There I ate a foul dinner of baked beans and tinned sausages, and thought about rats and methane gas – rats, because everyone I had met had warned me about their size and ferocity, and methane gas, because the back wall of the tent was six inches away from the mud in which *Magdalen* was wallowing. Curious scuttlings and sinister bubblings emanated from the canal . . .

The tent had been there for six months. Passers-by had grown used to it, and to the white boat moored at its side. British Waterways Board employees did nothing about it, as was their custom of old; day by day, the canvas frayed and the poles assumed more and more drunken angles. At last, there could be discerned through the gauzy material a shape as of a camp-bed with . . . something . . . lying on it in a formless huddle. It was a party of adventurous school children who first investigated; two hours later the police arrived. For on the camp-bed was a skeleton, and on the bones, like the marks of tiny chisels, were the scrapes of rats' teeth; hundreds, thousands, millions. 'He must have put up a good fight,' said the chief constable, eyeing the bones. 'But there was too many for him.'

'Ay, poor booger,' said the detective inspector against a counterpoint of retching constables. 'Orrible way to go.'

Leaping to my feet, I staggered out of the tent and went looking for human society. Since I had no Ordnance Survey map and it was pitch dark, it was hard to find. But after a five-mile walk through some of the blackest lanes human ingenuity could devise, I arrived under street lights. During the walk I had conceived a violent desire to speak to the loved ones at home. There were, however, no telephone boxes. Finally I tripped over a suburb of Bromsgrove, which proved to contain a public house. The building was seventeenth-century, with half-timbering restored by cunning hands to look as if it had been faked in 1956. The innkeeper dragged himself away from his conversation long enough to pull me a pint of mild. I asked him if he had a telephone.

'Yes,' he said, with that slow Midlands leer of hundred-and-one-proof complacency spreading across his simian features. 'And it's private.' Then he returned to his discourse, which was on the subject of blood clots. and Gina whose legs swole up. Somebody else had been having terrible deep pains in their legs. Someone else again was in the hospital, clot in foot, on one of them new computerized drips . . .

I walked back in a state of abject gloom. Somehow I had got on to the side of a dual carriageway, and I thought of thumbing a lift to somewhere I could talk to somebody I knew about something I was interested in. The fields were lined with ten-foot barbed wire fences on angled concrete posts. Everyone in the Midlands seemed to loathe and mistrust each other. What on earth was I *doing* in this appalling place?

I turned off the road, my flashlight lancing a long tube in the fog. I had no idea what I was doing. So why go on?

Ahead, the balance-beams of a lock gate winked into the flashlight's glow. This was encouraging; it suggested the way out.

'The reason I am here,' I said aloud, 'is to go on. The reason for going on is to go on.'

It sounded amazingly convincing at the time.

Rowing *Magdalen* on still water was proving extremely tiring. On the Severn, we had covered about thirty miles a day without difficulty. During my first two days on the canal, we had covered twenty; ten miles a day. It was not just the loss of speed while I was actually rowing. On the river, it had been possible to rest on the oars and be carried down the fastest part of the stream. If I did that on the canal, *Magdalen* crept sluggishly forward under her own momentum, wallowed to port and locked with the bankside vegetation. I was therefore rowing all the time; forty strokes a minute for eight hours, nearly twenty thousand strokes a day. This made locks feel positively restful.

I awoke feeling curiously shaky, drank coffee and crawled out of the tent. A single magpie flopped across lock forty-seven, vanishing across the foggy hillsides. As I packed up, my knees began to shake. They shook so badly that I had to sit down. It may have been malnutrition or nervous exhaustion. Whatever it was, for twenty minutes I moved around my patch of thistles on all fours, so weak that it took five goes to open my breakfast corned beef. After breakfast I felt stronger, packed up and started up the locks.

At the third lock, the windlass slipped from my nerveless fingers while I was letting down a paddle, flew off and dealt me a blow on the upper arm which paralysed the whole works for half an hour. In addition, the locks themselves were in an abominable state of repair, their upper gates leaking great gouts of water into the chamber, *Magdalen*'s bottom, and, once the curse of the Midlands had really got going, the pockets of my waterproof coat. This I did not discover until it began to rain and I put my hand in my pocket for my camera.

My argument with myself the previous night had not been conclusive. I was still wrapped in deep gloom, which was heightened by the general sense of shakiness that had overcome me. Part of the trouble was that the canal section of the journey seemed to be passing with agonizing slowness. At this rate I could be plodding on for ten days or more, and I was by no means sure that flesh and blood could bear it. Cars whizzed across a bridge ahead. Any of them could have been at my home in an hour and a quarter. Yet it had taken a week to get this far . . .

'Shut up,' I told myself. For this was recognizably the spirit of the Bure disaster. What I needed, and needed desperately, was (I realized) a packet of peanuts. A cunning blend of protein, salt, and monosodium glutamate. (I craved salt. Perhaps the shaking was because of a shortage of the stuff.)

The next obstacle on the list was the Tardebigge tunnel, through which, the BWB had informed me, I was under no circumstances allowed to proceed in a small boat. Possibly, I thought, there might be a shop or public house at the mouth of the tunnel, at which peanuts could be secured. There was no pub or shop. (Though there was a large British Waterways Board maintenance yard, several of whose employees watched with interest as I steered *Magdalen* into the mouth of the tunnel.)

This time, the tunnel was easier, though longer. You may remember that in the film of *The Dam Busters* the pilots gauged their height by shining lights on the water. I suppose it was the condition of the Tardebigge locks that put me in mind of the film; whatever it was, before entering the tunnel I jammed a powerful flashlight pointing upwards and slightly astern, and wedged it with two tins of baked beans and the binoculars. This created a spot of light on the tunnel roof directly at the centre line of the boat. Provided I kept it in line with the tunnel entrance (and provided nobody came steaming through in the opposite direction) this significantly enhanced my prospects of survival. Feats of technical wizardry notwithstanding, the passage of the Tardebigge was still a hazardous business, and materially increased the craving for peanuts. The reader will therefore imagine my disappointment at discovering no public house at the far end, either. It later transpired that bargees in the nineteenth century were in the habit of preparing themselves for the rigours of the tunnel by drinking a bottle or two of gin at the boozers which, in those days, stood one at each end. Since their only means of progress was by lying on a plank, one each side of their boat's bows, and 'legging' or walking the boat through with their feet, it is not surprising that those of them who were drunk not infrequently fell in, and drowned. An Earl of Plymouth who owned the land on which the pubs were built had them both torn down in order to save bargees misery, little knowing that in the far future he would be depriving a pioneer of peanuts. History is certainly pretty ironic stuff.

After the tunnel, and another one shortly after that, the canal ran among plantations of beech and larch, still with most of their leaves on and with great skeins of mist caught in their branches and rides. Three fallow deer sprinted off down a path; season of mists and mellow fruitfulness, I thought, running into a reeking diesel slick. The slick stretched as far as the marina at Alvechurch, where the peanut famine came to an end in a public bar, as did the steak-and-kidney pie famine. The landlord was playing the Portsmouth Sinfonia at full volume. An elderly man with a white face and bluish lips talked to me for a long time. I could not understand what he was saying; he seemed to be telling me he had been in hospital and had three somethings out. The Portsmouth Sinfonia stopped, but by this time I could not think of any organs in the human body that occur in threes; and speculation made it difficult to concentrate. He soon lit a cigarette and had a coughing fit, so I bought him a milk stout and made my farewells. Outside the pub I met John Sargent, a lock-keeper. He had a jovial red face and assured me that I would never get through the Wast Hill Tunnel. Then he darted away before I could make him explain.

The morning had been autumnal and sunny. Now the sun had slid behind a cloud, and the sunset had begun. It was only two o'clock; night was not scheduled to come down for at least another four hours. Nonetheless the clouds were scarlet and gold, rays of light shot from the heavens as if in some celestial motion-picture theatre, and a chilly breeze began rattling the bankside vegetation. It was all most puzzling.

Half an hour later, it looked the same, more Wagnerian, if anything. Even the fishermen had disappeared from the scene. The hills were upon us: the canal plunged between the banks of a deep cutting. At the summit of the cutting was a corrugated-iron shed of vaguely agricultural aspect, from which seeped a smell the like of which I have only ever experienced when once, while hitchhiking, I got a lift in a horse butcher's van that had not been scrubbed for six weeks.

As the banks became lower, the colour of the water was changing. Ever since the Severn it had been a pleasing grey-green. Now it was black and completely opaque, so that if you stuck your finger in it the finger looked as if it had been amputated. There was no habitation on the banks, but rubbish was beginning to gather; a dead refrigerator here, an upturned perambulator there. Then a couple of houses crept close enough to the river to reveal, in the garden of one of them, a huge cabin cruiser. Round the garden ran a wall of concrete blocks with a two-foot-six wicket gate. It looked like Gabriel Garcia Marquez's galleon in the jungle, left by some prehistoric incursion of the sea.

Past a pub the banks began to rise again, until the daylight was a slit of red and gold, and the thorn trees lining the towpath were yellow-leaved in a way that suggested not autumn, but a total absence of light from one year's end to the next. Far above, a bridge spanned the cutting in one elegant arch. It was not the ordinary, workmanlike canal bridge. This was a landscape architect's poem in brick, flung across the cutting to show people what he could do when he really set his mind to it. And at the end of the cutting, looking small and insignificant at the vanishing point of the banks, was the entrance to the Wast Hill tunnel.

The Wast Hill tunnel was, in its time, one of the wonders of the engineering world. It is 2,726 yards long, and when it was begun in July 1794 the idea excited general derision. It was finished in April 1797, to the amazement of all concerned (including, it seems, the shareholders). The bridges at either end are a celebration of the achievement.

Wast Hill is trouble.

The atmosphere of the place was sinister to a degree. Previous tunnels had also stared balefully, but they had been short enough for their far ends to be visible. This one was matt black, an eye without a pupil. From it there blew a cold wind bearing a stink of sulphuric acid that stung the tear ducts. There was a slight current in the water; on it rode pieces of broken furniture and old polythene bags and magazines from whose covers heavy-breasted young ladies leered, adjusting their stocking tops and flopping with the ripples. The Wast Hill tunnel is known to poetic souls as the gateway to the Black Country. If this was the gateway, I did not fancy the thing itself.

I have to confess that cowardice now overcame me. I rowed back the way I had come, quarrelling furiously with myself. The dialogue, between the intrepid explorer and the cow'rin tim'rous beastie, went something like this:

CTB: Look, there's no end in sight, there may be boats coming, and if you meet one you've had it. That tunnel is only sixteen feet wide. A narrow boat is seven feet wide. None of those hire-boat drivers knows how to steer. Also, think of your wife and children.

IE: So what? I've got an excellent flashlight. Look, I've changed the batteries. If there's a boat coming, we can cower under the wall. As to wife and children, you are of course heavily insured.

CTB (*feebly*): Of course. But it's not just the – er – money. Yes, what a nice torch. But if we meet someone, how do we know it won't be a hire boat with one of those drunk people steering it?

IE: Yellow rat. (*Pause*) See what you mean. Good Lord, dash it all, man, have you the guts of a teeny worm? We'll try it anyway. Better to die—

CTB: No! No, no, no, no, and again no. Besides, it's against the law. And that John Sargent bloke, the lock-keeper. He said you'd never—

IE (*caving in*): You will be ashamed of this decision, spineless oaf.

And of course I was. *Magdalen* and I returned to the mouth of the tunnel, where I fished a copy of *Swank* out of the briny and peered listlessly at the sodden cuties for a hour. Possibly a boat would come up, and we would get a tow.

No boat came.

Familiarity began breeding contempt.

I rowed to the mouth of the tunnel and listened. Water slapped and boomed in the echoes. There did not seem to be any engines. I lodged the flashlight in the picnic basket and rowed in, singing, as far as I can remember, 'The Ram of Derby'. From inside the entrance was grey because of the lack of light in the cutting. Slowly, it began to shrink. After a while, the song changed to 'Nearer, My God, To Thee'. The yellow coin of the flashlight's beam wavered on the roof: black and red brick, dripping; glistening grey organ pipes of nitre. I turned my head to look forwards. It was so dark that I could not even tell if I was looking in the right direction. I had stopped singing some time previously. When I coughed, the echoes roared around me. A phrase from an old poem echoed in my mind: 'Sod this for a game of skittles,' it ran.

Turning around, I pulled as fast as I could for the open air.

★

I waited another hour. High above, the sunset continued unabated; eventually, the world began to darken. A boat came out of the tunnel. A blonde woman was standing at the tiller. She looked pale. They had been motoring for twenty minutes in that tunnel, she said. For ten of those minutes she had not been able to see either end.

Slowly, I pulled back down the canal and put up the tent between a couple of thorn bushes. After supper, I smote the gas lamp with my head, breaking the mantle. There were no spares, so I trudged back to the pub to write my diary. The public bar was full of men telling each other dirty jokes and grinning. They had whippets with them. The whippets grinned too. So did the gin traps that a man was selling to another man under a table. Oh yes, everything was grinning.

Except me.

I was woken the next morning by a bird of ill omen standing on my tent and cursing in Modern Greek. By the time I had achieved full consciousness, I had fallen off the camp-bed in my sleeping bag and was wriggling among the debris like a giant maggot. It was pitch dark, and extremely early.

It was now plain that the only way of getting through the Wast Hill tunnel was by hitchhiking. So I rowed down to a bridge by the pub, where the canal narrowed and boats coming through would cut their speed. On the bridge was a notice board, half-visible in the early light. It said that dire penalties lay in store for people defacing or damaging fences or works, shooting or propelling any stone, shot, bullet or other missile or throwing refuse, live or dead animals into the canal.

'Prisoner at the bar. You have confessed that on 11 October you did take up your station on the canal bank, demolishing divers blades of grass with your stool; that you did wantonly and with malice aforethought project into the canal handfuls of maggots and breadcrumbs; and that you did throughout the day bombard this innocent and placid piece of water with lead shot and twisted spikes of barbed metal. Have you anything to say for yourself?'

'I was fishing, m'Lud. Honest—'

'Take it out and shoot it. Next case.'

The light grew. My feet were getting cold. What if no one came? The boat was too heavy to carry round, and in the absence of a towing vehicle there was nothing to do but sit and read sodden pornography that I already knew by heart.

This was tedious, since it was early in the morning and the mind, not yet warmed up for the day, turned on solemn matters like what would be frying on the stove at home at that moment. Nothing but edginess could come of this. I wished I had a book to read, but all my books were shut up in the container, which was only openable on dry land. I could have landed, but I knew that as soon as I had the boat unpacked, a hitchable craft would surge around the corner, and that by the time I had repacked, it would have gone. Besides, the only books I had brought were *Three Men in a Boat,* the *Diary of a Rowing Tour in 1875* and a lot of other inland waterways books, and frankly I did not wish to be reminded about inland waterways just at the moment. So I sat and decided that what would be on the stove was sausages, bacon, tomatoes, a few kidneys and some scrambled egg, not forgetting a pot of coffee and a large quantity of toast made with decent brown bread, not Mother's Pride—

There was a whirr like a sewing machine from the far side of the bridge. Rapidly, I pulled into hitchhiking position, bang across the centre of the thoroughfare. As I raised my thumb I noticed it was still bright blue. The narrow boat slowed to take evasive action. I looped my towline round its after bollards. Then I said, 'Could you possibly give me a tow through the tunnel?'

They looked slightly dazed, at first – as was perfectly understandable, it not being usual on hire-boat holidays to be accosted by ragged blue people in very old white boats. The tunnel approached and swallowed us up. The roof poured water. The entrance shrank to the size of a pinprick, and disappeared. There was no sign of the exit. My host said it reminded him of Geoffrey Howe, this tunnel. Sopping wet. Yes, I said. And no light visible at the end. How we roared. You have to remember that it was not yet half-past eight in the morning.

But after a while the laughter died away. The spotlight on the narrow boat's bow lit brick and filthy water. The engine roared, and streams of water splattered from the roof. Astern, the entrance vanished. Ahead, there was only more blackness. How long had we been in the tunnel? My host said twenty minutes, and laughed nervously when his wife told him it was only ten.

As last, a grey dot showed ahead. Nobody wanted to seem too eager, but everyone was quite evidently relieved that this tube really *had* an exit. As it became obvious that this was indeed the far end, the conversation swelled and became jolly again, and we all laughed and listened to the echoes mix with the engine noise. And as we came into daylight, we discovered that, having entered the tunnel as chance acquaintances, we had emerged good friends. They gave me coffee and offered me a tow as far as the junction with the Stratford Canal. But our emergence into daylight had blown away the gloom of the past forty-eight hours, and I declined, saying that I would row it and do the thing properly. (I suppose I was partially insane, by this time.) They all looked respectful, as if acknowledging that a man had to do what a man had to do. I gave Twix bars to their children, and they pulled away, taking photographs.

Onward, into the throbbing heart of the Midlands!

The Stratford-on-Avon Canal conveys visions of apple cheeks, magpie-timbered cottages fighting for survival under their burdens of honeysuckle, and public houses selling mulled ale with bits of toast in it. The reality is somewhat different.

The canal begins about a mile north of the Wast Hill Tunnel. You pick your way through the bedsteads and disused Ford Cortinas with which the Worcester and Birmingham is decorated. On the left, the fine spire of King's Norton Church rises from a mat of grubby semis. You feel rather relieved that you are not going to be continuing on the Worcester and Birmingham, because Birmingham is just beginning to happen, and if the water gets any dirtier you fear it will eat the paint off the boat. (There is rumoured to be patch of water in a canal somewhere in Birmingham which is so clear that you can count every spoke on every pram wheel on the bottom at a depth of six feet. The clarity is apparently due to the fact that it is so poisonous that even filth cannot survive it.)

Just as matters look as if they may become seriously unpleasant, a channel of black water opens out to the right. This is the way to Stratford. There is a signpost there. If, as seems likely, the signpost has been demolished by vandals next time you go, you will be able to tell you are in the right place when you see a soot-black wall bearing the inscription BLACK SCUM GET OUT OF BRUM. Further along, there are more carefully-thought-out segments of British Movement philosophy. YOU ARE NOW ENTERING A WHITE ZONE, one of them says.

In the white zone of the Stratford-on-Avon Canal, autumn was a month further advanced than in the rest of the country. The leaves were yellow, as if with a liver complaint. The tree trunks, in defiance of the British Movement, were black. So was the water. Under the trees there were soggy copies of the *Sun* and old tin cans. Under the concrete bridges there were more inscriptions, giving intimate physical details of what Noddy did to Brenda there. The towpath and much of the surrounding area were inches deep in smashed bottles. If you want to find Noddy or Brenda to congratulate them, you will know who they are without being introduced because at least one of them will have knees cut to ribbons by broken glass.

It was a peculiar place, this white zone. Extraordinarily inefficiently run. for one thing. If one knew who it was who policed it, one would write them a stiffish letter pointing out its shortcomings, foremost among which was the fact that there was nothing white about it. The sky was grey. The water was black. The factories backing on to the canal were red, the foam from their effluent yellow. I have already mentioned the leaves, yellow too. The treetrunks and indeed almost everything else was black. It would have been interesting to check out the people, but unfortunately there were none to be seen.

The only flesh and blood was a series of huge Alsatians, the Midlands' favourite pet, whose teeth were undeniably white, as well as being long, sharp and bared. Several of these tried to rush up my oar and eat me, possibly because I was blue. Or possibly because the white zone is an Alsatian reserve, a sort of collecting point or Alsatian pool supplying the surrounding counties, in which all humans have long ago passed down the pink gullets of their four-legged acquaintances. Someone, not me, should look into this. Personally, I chose to travel as rapidly as was consistent with repelling canine boarders with great glittering sweeps of my cutlass. It is probably wise when passing through this zone to take a sub-machine-gun or a good lump of raw meat and a supply of strychnine. Though it must be said that there is no good reason for going there, unless you are trying to get round the bottom of Birmingham and on to the Grand Union Canal.

As I left the white zone it started to rain, which, though unpleasant, seemed appropriate. Houses, dead trees, derelict cars and power pylons all dripped. At lunchtime a man on the bank raised a drawbridge for me. So I bought him a drink in a brand-new pub in what was beginning to be an acceptable-type suburb. He was a trainee butcher who had just left school. He was the only person I met on the trip who seemed to wish that he was doing it too; but he reckoned it was the job that mattered, so of course it was all for the best, and it was indoors and dry, ho, ho, at least. Except, he said, sadly, staring with his doggy brown eyes at the inch of beer left in his glass, that when he had been at school he had always liked being out in the rain, alone.

Personally I was not so keen.

The canal crawled over an aqueduct and into flat Warwickshire countryside. The sky got lower, and the rain kept falling, and everything got wetter and wetter. Someone had called their cabin cruiser *Beau Lox*.

A wind arose, blowing from the direction I was heading. The canal had a faint current, in the wrong direction, full of dying leaves. It may be that the stars in their courses were against me, but of course I was in no position to confirm or deny this since the cloud cover was total, and low enough to obliterate the upper branches of canalside trees. The mind rambled away; the hat brim dripped on to the nose; blue dye dripped from the hands on to the PVC trousers, from there on to the camera, from the camera on to the maps, from the maps on to the biscuits, and from the

[115]

biscuits into the bottom of the boat. As the afternoon wore on, the bottom of the boat became less and less well-defined, as maps, biscuits and other less identifiable objects and substances combined to form a gummy mass in the bilges.

The canals of England are with a few exceptions cared for by the British Waterways Board, or BWB. The BWB issues licenses to those wishing to travel on navigable waterways. It charges fees for these licenses. With the proceeds, it is supposed to keep locks working, canals watertight, and generally to ensure that boats can start at A and arrive at B without having to be carried more than, say, two miles in every ten. And it does a terrific job, despite lack of finance, and manpower. Its sole detectable weakness is that it gives the impression that it does not particularly want its canals used by anyone. One seems to hear it asking peevishly why people insist on rushing around in boats when they could simply drive to a nearby lay-by and take a short walk to the towpath, where they could make a few respectful noises before driving off about their business.

At about four o'clock, I had decided that the locks must be drawing nigh. I was dragging along in a deep trance of misery when the sound of engines came from round a bend. Twenty seconds later, I observed a British Waterways Board barge nosing rustily towards me. Working boats have right of way, so I scuttled for a notch in the bank and jammed *Magdalen* into it with an oar.

As the barge came on, it grew. There were two of them, one ahead of and one behind a small tugboat. They were lashed together rigidly, rather than flexibly; the overall length of the unit was perhaps a hundred and sixty feet, loaded to the gunwales with slime dredged from the canal floor. It was wonderful to watch, this mighty engine travelling on a canal designed for boats seventy feet long. What skill, I thought, like threading a needle or being a Space Invaders champion. The rusty snout of the front barge was pointing straight at me. I waited for it to swing away.

It didn't.

And that would have been that, if I hadn't had an oar overboard, lodged in the canal bed. The mental picture that remains is of that oar bending until looked like a wishbone and was hard against *Magdalen*'s side, and then of *Magdalen*'s side bending three inches inwards. This picture fades out, to be replaced by the sound of my own voice, raised, reasoning with the half-witted gorilla at the controls of his juggernaut. After that, receding engine and pouring rains and *Magdalen* leaking like a basket.

If ever I see a BWB man chugging around a harbour in a barge, and I am driving an ocean liner, he had better have his crash helmet and waterwings ready.

The Lapworth flight of locks runs down from the Birmingham plateau towards a valley whose name I would certainly tell you if I could read it, but which is on a part of the map that has unfortunately not survived the inundations of that dreadful evening. Crazed with rage and exhaustion, I staggered blindly through the first twelve of the locks. *Magdalen* was stumbling too, resembling not so much a boat as a mobile pond. My boots skidded on mossy concrete and glassy lock gates. It was getting dark; there was nowhere to camp because a main road ran on the left, and on the right, thickets of bramble and hawthorn cowered under the lashing downpour. Normally this would have been worrying. Not this time; since yesterday there was no such thing as a rational thought. The only driving factor was to be somewhere other than where I was at the particular moment I was thinking about it. Never mind that in half an hour it was going to be pitch dark and I was going to fall into a lock and be recovered from the paddles some weeks later, horribly mangled; Death, one began to mumble in cracked, hysterical tones, where was thy sting?

It was at this point that a voice said, 'Hello.'

It belonged to John Sargent, the lock-keeper. This time he had on his ministering angel hat. He took one look at my rolling eye and flooded boat and went back to his house to fetch his son. Together they helped me down the locks, opening gates and paddles, and making soothing conversation. The boy was a Wolf Cub. He had his own boat and seemed to be looking forward to the day when he had drunk the regulation lockful of water and could claim to be a fully-fledged canal person. The father had become a lock-keeper to avoid going into the family business: between the lines, I sensed the baffled rage of Midlands conformists against the pariah. He spoke of the decision half-ruefully, half-proudly, rather as if it was a prison sentence for a crime he didn't mind admitting to. He said that there was hot water in the lock house if I wanted it, and showed me a tiny garden with twelve-foot hedges where I could pitch the tent. I turned down the hot water, as I would probably have been unable to hold back my emotion. But the garden was a miracle, since it was now blowing force eight. The tent went up, then half-way down again, bending under the weight of wet clothes. The atmosphere inside it was London Particular, condensing on all metal objects, including the brass point of a biro. I headed out.

In the pub down the locks, an Alsatian ate three ploughman's lunches, including the pickled onions. A vivacious lady from Solihull, wearing tight dungarees, was getting stewed on Mateus Rosé at the bar. She sounded like Shula Archer. In the gents, the local Lions Club clanked with metal regalia. They were making humorous remarks in rotation, then laughing politely in unison. Back in the bar Shula Archer had fallen off her stool and the Alsatian was doing awful damage to a bag of pork scratchings.

Outside it was raining drops that were only just bigger than fog, warm and not so much falling as drifting. Then, as I was preparing to dive into the tent, the clouds went off the sky like the edge of a huge black blanket, and the stars came out like diamonds sewn on velvet.

CHAPTER SEVEN

Lapworth to Napton

Antipodean waterfolk – The Grand Union Canal – Cassandra on the Hatton flight – Home from home under the Warwick bypass – A tragic tale of life and death – Escape from Leamington Spa – The Warwickshire Fly Boat Company – I become a back cabin bargee – An appointment with Destiny – My pleas avail

The morning was clear as crystal, with a fingernail of old moon hanging among the fading stars. The sun flooded the sky with lemon yellow as I took the tent down; there was no breath of wind. According to the weather forecast, the Stratford-on-Avon Canal was at this very moment shuddering under hail and torrential rain, impelled by force-nine gales and lit by frequent shafts of lightning. *Magdalen* was half-full of water. I put in a couple of plugs of plastic padding (the craftsman's friend) where the British Waterways Board had holed her, and it was with a feeling of slickness, crispness and good will to all men that we set off down the first lock.

It was not yet eight in the morning – a time of the day at which human emotions are susceptible to sudden and violent upsets. Also, by the feel of it, the curious, half-rotten moods of *Magdalen*s.

It was pleasant to see, at the third lock down, a woman with blonde hair and large teeth winding up the paddles. We were in the second lock at the time. She trotted up the towpath and we exchanged good mornings. Then she looked down into the chamber, where *Magdalen* was sinking towards the level of the downhill pound. There was a moment's silence. Then her laugh rang through the still of the morning, rattling windows as far away as Warwick.

'That tiny little thing!' she cried, bracingly. 'You're using a whole lockful of water for . . . that tiny little thing!'

By her accent, she came from Australia. I therefore asked her how long she had been over from New Zealand. (You will observe from this hideous insult delivered to a perfect stranger that it was indeed very early in the morning.) She pretended not to have heard. *Magdalen* lay and glowered in the bottom of the lock, obviously restraining herself only with difficulty from making some cultured remark about convicts.

We emerged from our respective locks. Mrs Australia returned, still neighing, to her boat. Mr Australia came to take her place. He gazed patronizingly at *Magdalen*' and said, 'Ah. An old clinker,' as if discussing furnace slag. After that he asked how much she was worth. I said, oh, three or four thousand pounds, and he said that you could get one like it for about a twentieth of that in Australia. I explained that she was very, very, ancient, having been built in 1899, and he gave a short, sceptical, nasty laugh. It seemed to be time to change the subject.

The Australian had come to London a couple of months ago, after two years in the tropics. Since then he had been living in an hotel room with his wife and two children. One began to understand why he seemed slightly jaundiced. They had hired a narrow boat for a bit of privacy, he said; it was nice to see a bit of rain and get some peace and quiet, because the kids were driving him round the bend.

Yes, I said, winding up a paddle.

He watched the boiling water, looking slightly awestruck. Then, with a return to his old abrasive form, he asked me what I thought I was doing, using up all that water for a tiny little boat. No doubt after his time in the tropics he had the whole thing costed out at so many notes the gallon. His wife shrieked at him that breakfast was ready and we parted, he observing that in his view there was no way I'd get that thing (here *Magdalen* lurched in the water, and would have had his leg off had she not been ten feet down in a lock) through the big locks on the Grand Union. An encouraging person. So I encouraged him with the news that there was a sleeping sickness epidemic upstream, and that if he wished to avoid it he should dust his sheets with powdered sugar before retiring.

At the bottom of the Lapworth flight, the Stratford passes within a few hundred yards of the Grand Union. There is a short link between them, known as Kingswood Junction. Passing from the

Stratford on to the Grand Union is like coming out of an abandoned coalmine into the Paris Metro.

It connects Birmingham with London, where one of its arms enters the Thames at Limehouse, and the other at Brentford. Until 1929 it was a jumble of short canals owned by a variety of different companies. In 1929 it was taken over by the Grand Union Canal Company, and beginning in 1932, was modernized, widened, deepened, and generally gussied up until the money ran out, which, as usually happens in canal schemes, was not long afterwards. It was designed to speed up narrow boat traffic; the locks were enlarged so the boats could enter two abreast. The locks themselves hold about 98,000 gallons each, which was one of the things that seemed to be preparing the Australian person for his brain haemorrhage.

The move on to the broad placid, surface of the GU from the narrow, gale-whipped writhings of the Stratford marked an epoch on the journey. I was now, according to my previous night's calculations, halfway to London! The fact that these calculations were wrong did not diminish the joy of the moment.

For from now on, *things could only get better* (unless *Magdalen* sank, and somehow that did not come into the reckoning). I had been ten days on the water. I was fit as a Boat Race oar, I had plenty of supplies, and I could (as I then thought) get no wetter. All systems were functioning perfectly. Shame overcame me that a mere two days ago I had been thinking of caving in and heading for home. Moment of weakness, I told myself; the spell of the Midlands. But now everything was coming up roses. Ten more days to Westminster! And between here and Westminster, only the Grand Union Canal, the Oxford Canal, and the Thames. A pleasant glide through a decreasingly industrialized landscape; a pastoral idyll; and then the home of pleasure boating. No more wild Wales and roaring Severn and industrial Midlands. We were on the home straight.

Or so I thought, fool that I was. Cocky fool.

Grand Union is not an encouraging name; it has a nasty ring of the Victorian workhouse. An exploratory mission, conducted from the windows of a Euston-bound 125 train, had revealed a blur of muddy water snaking through tedious countryside. It was therefore rather a shock to glide out on to a mighty artery of brown water, to twitch the right oar and to be borne along past crisp, well-tended banks by a warm but powerful wind which for once was blowing from dead astern.

The cut ran along the side of a sunlit hill, from which distant thunderstorms could be seen billowing over faraway lowlands as per forecast. Herds of fat white bullocks browsed on the uphill bank. A buzzard wheeled on steep-angled wings over a timbered barnyard. A sparrow hawk hurtled down the wind, pivoted with the flick of a wing, and vanished in a flash of grey over a beech wood. Just before lunchtime, we passed a butty boat, tied up next to a formal garden on the canal bank. (A butty boat is a narrow boat without an engine. Originally, narrow boats travelled in pairs. It is the butty boat that has the huge, brilliantly painted rudder, crusted with carving and pipeclayed sinnet.) After the butty was a bridge. After the bridge were the Hatton locks, all twenty of them, one after the other.

From the top lock, there is a wonderful view across the depths of the Avon valley, with the tower of St Mary's, Warwick rising in their midst. The view is the last shred of the Grand Union idyll, for the time being.

The importance of Hatton can be judged from the fact that it possesses two lock-keepers and a shed with a sinister hole into which you can pump out your Elsan, should you so desire. One of the lock-keepers came and helped me through seven or eight locks. (BWB lock-keepers are uniformly kind and helpful, unlike BWB maintenance men who seem to be selected for genetic closeness to gorillas with indigestion.) As he wound paddles up and down with the windlass that he kept hooked in his black leather belt, he reminisced about the old days. Once the Hatton maintenance yard had a hundred men. During the industrial holiday they would service two locks a day, descending on them like Puerto Ricans at a New York car wash, damming them off by dropping heavy planks into the grooves in the masonry, and keeping them pumped dry with pumps which until 1930 were made entirely of wood. Nowadays there are only a handful of men at Hatton, and if a lock goes wrong they service it then and there and if anyone wants to get past, too bad.

If you meet someone in a peaked cap and blue overalls near an inland waterway and you wish to find out whether or not he is a lock-keeper, there are certain standard tests. The first of these is to check cap colour. If it has a shiny black peak, the odds are good. If you can get him to turn around, check the back of the blue overalls for the word WATERWAYS in letters three inches high. If for some reason he refuses to turn around, make him sit down on a chair. If he screams it is because the windlass he is wearing in the belt across the small of his back has just been driven into his kidney.

Lock-keepers are great chatters. Anything is grist to their mill, though there is a noticeable tendency to gloom. This expresses itself both in fits of depression about the future of the canals (wouldn't be surprised if they was all bloody skateboard tracks twenty years from now) to the spreading of rumours about other canals.

We were walking down the locks when I noticed that one of the pounds was rather low. I remarked on the fact.

'Yes,' he said. 'It's got a leak.'

I observed that the water seemed low all over.

'It is,' he said. 'The Oxford Canal's closed now, unless you've got a mooring on it.' He turned his head. 'You all right?' he said.

'Fine,' I said, when I had regained my breath. The Oxford Canal closed? I would be cut off from the Thames; there was no route down the Grand Union, even if I wanted to take it, because the Blisworth tunnel was closed. I was stuck. 'Completely closed?' I said.

'No water in the summit level,' said the keeper.

'Would they let me up? Only I've got to get to London,' I said weakly.

'You might talk 'em round,' he said. 'There again, you might not.'

Gloom descended, accompanied by a faint, mocking scent of roses.

Towards the bottom of the flight, two old ladies were winding up a paddle very slowly, using two windlasses at a time. Further down, *Magdalen*, fed up with crashing against lock walls, sank all the rope fenders I had carefully made for her, and floated away in the middle of a large, mud-fringed pound. A fisherman lent me his landing-net handle to retrieve her. He said it was the first time he had ever spoken to anyone in a boat. Normally boats were a pain in the neck and in fact he was surprised at himself, if he'd had time to think he would have let it drift out to sea.

There is a small patch of brambles on the outskirts of Warwick. Above it, the A6 and the A41 roar with delight as they intersect. In the middle of it, a small stopcock smells faintly of gas. The towpath runs past it, sprinkled with glittering shards of broken glass. On it, that night, I erected first the tent and then the fly-sheet. Then I laid my sheet of industrial polythene inside it, erected the camp-bed and disposed the necessities of life in their accustomed places. Then I went in, made sure the machete was ready to hand, and gave myself over to suspense. There was nothing I could do but wait and see.

Leamington Spa is a fine example of a community that uses its canal to the full. Many shortsighted wet liberal communities use canals as linear parks, amenity stripes, urban lungs and *rus in urbe*. Not the Spa, though one can in spots detect some bureaucratic gestures towards greenness, mainly in the form of corrugated-iron fences. They realize that the object of a canal is to be a repository for junk, and they work at it with grim determination.

You will remember that in *Three Men in a Boat*, the author discourses at length on the corpse of a poor young woman that he and his companions have pulled out of the river. As I pulled past the wrecked frigidaires and pedal cars of Leamington, I was reflecting that what I needed was an event of this calibre. Something to pluck at the heart strings, to exorcize if possible the scuzzy spell of the Midlands, and to distract me from fruitless self-torture about the Oxford Canal. Then, looking over my shoulder, I espied something blue protruding from a pile of tin cans on the surface. The tin cans bobbed aside on my wake, to reveal . . . a shiny, this-year's model Honda moped.

It was the old tale. An owner who worked down the fridge factory and bought her on the drip. For as long as the payments lasted, it was all roses; oil on the chain, twelve-to-one in the tank. But then came the first dividend. For a week or so there was no oil in the two-stroke and his face was flushed with drink, and his heavy boot bruised her delicate chain-case cruelly. And after that he fell off her, twice, and hit her soft blue enamel with his big fat cigar; and then, one fatal day, he rode her carelessly down to Ernie's Older Fords and paid cash for a '76 Cortina. He drove away without looking back. She lurked against a wall all day, hoping he would remember. That night there came shabby boys with spiky hair and huge boots, and they dragged her into a playground and abused her until her cams and gears burned like fire and she spluttered to a halt for shame. And then they took her, that innocent oriental maid, and who knows what memories of her little slant-eyed manufacturers must have raced before her front forks as they threw her, glinting in the light of their Woolies pocket flashlights, into the canal . . .

The climb out of the Avon valley means more locks. There are compensations, however; you are getting away from Leamington Spa, for one thing. For another, you have left the industrial Midlands behind. The water changes from muck-brown to an attractive blue-green-grey, the colour of Samantha Eggar's eyes. The broken glass content of the towpath falls to about one per cent. Ink-cap mushrooms grow beside the locks; the lock-keeper's cottages, long since sold off by the BWB, are beautifully kept. Even the locks are interesting. One of them had two chambers, without an intervening pound. The total rise must have been twenty feet, about ten feet per gate. It was theoretically possible for a really creative traveller to fill up both locks to the top and then to release the paddles on the topmost one, thereby creating in rural Warwickshire an effect halfway between Niagara Falls and the cascade at the Villa d'Este. Above the lock five kingfishers were behaving like a turquoise necklace being torn apart by poltergeists.

A few miles up the canal, you come to Long Itchington, a village in the heart of the Blue Lias, the clay from which bricks are made and in which the bones of dinosaurs are found. It was dusk by the time I arrived at Long Itchington bottom lock. The previous day, I had been told by a narrow-boat person to drop in for a cup of tea. After Long Itchington Bridge, she had said. First boat on the left. But after Long Itchington Bridge there was only the usual slab of black water, not a boat in sight. Feeling rather depressed, I started on up through the locks.

At the bottom of the second lock, I looked up. There above me was the stern of a narrow boat. It was a singularly beautiful narrow boat, black-and-brass chimney on its back cabin, owner's name in the looping fairground script beloved of narrow-boat fiends. A shower of golden sparks drifted out over the lower pound, accompanied by the whine of a grindstone. Opening the lock gates, I pulled *Magdalen* in. She rose smoothly into a new world.

The pound was full of narrow boats. There were black derelicts, slumped at their moorings; stripped hulks, bare metal and red lead; conversions, boxed-in and many-windowed; and work boats, crisp with surgeon-green tarpaulins over their empty holds, their elegant back cabins painted with roses and castles, red and yellow diamonds, and hung with snow-white lanyards of Turk's-head and square sinnet. And above it all, the black-and-gold stovepipes, wafting feathers of woodsmoke at an indigo sky fringed with black trees.

A sign by the canalside said, The Warwickshire Fly Boat Company. Men, mostly youngish and bearded, were wandering around with paint pots and welding torches and bits of timber. There were many dogs. Everyone ignored me except the dogs, which barked furiously. I had the sensation of intruding into a closed world, like a brush salesman in a Trappist monastery. Panicking, I gave the oars a brisk twitch and sailed towards the next lock.

'Hullo,' said a voice from the middle hatch of a long tar-black conversion. 'Fancy a cup of tea?' The voice belonged to Ginny Sloper, the narrow boat person. I had met her on the Hatton flight bustling round with a windlass and two narrow boats lashed side-by-side. I tied up astern of her boat, and went aboard.

Ginny inhabits a conversion, which means a working-boat hull on to which a boxy superstructure has been grafted. In the saloon was a small but red-hot coal stove and a gigantic Alsatian. I sat down in an armchair and she gave me tea and we chatted about this and that.

Beyond the window, night was falling over the canal. I was meant to be shuddering in my tent. Instead, I was hearing about the innermost secrets of the narrow-boat world from a beautiful woman in conditions of sinful luxury, viz. a cut moquette armchair, a hot stove, and a warm Alsatian on the feet. The lack of suffering induced guilt. Leaping on to the Alsatian, I dealt my head a painful blow on the ceiling, and said I had to go and find a place to put my tent. She said I could stay in the back cabin if I wanted to. No further persuasion was necessary.

There is a strong sense of caste in the narrow-boat world. Hire-boat drivers are untouchables. At the summit are those who inhabit seventy-foot boats. built for work in the days when the canals were a going concern. But even here there are distinctions. It is *infra dig* to inhabit a conversion on which the cargo space has been boxed in to provide living accommodation. Conversion dwellers are looked down on by haughty people with beards and grindstones. The true Brahmin lives on a work boat lovingly restored to better than its original condition, its cargo space draped in green tarpaulins. He eats, sleeps, cooks and washes in the back cabin, a tiny cave of Edwardian parlour kitsch. If he wants to make quite sure of his next incarnation, he may once a year take a load of coal for a ride on the canals, selling it as he goes at what usually amounts to a considerable loss. Then he presumably spends the rest of the year scrubbing out the boat. This is not common, however. Mostly, the Brahmin sits in his back cabin sustained by the social security and peering over his holy books. There is a strong affinity with train spotters here. Through study and self-denial it is possible to know the name, number and location of every narrow boat afloat in the British Isles. The difference between train spotters and narrow-boat fiends is that very few train spotters live in the cabs of steam locomotives.

Ginny was in the process of selling her conversion so she could buy a work boat. Later, I repaired to the back cabin, and got an idea of what such purists are in for. As in many other forms of spiritual discipline, mortification of the flesh plays an important part.

The back cabin is about seven feet long by five foot six inches wide. You go in through double doors, down a precipitous flight of steps. On your left is a coal range, from the Columbia stove works. Above the range are bars for drying clothes. Below it is a space in which wet boots can be grilled. Next to the range is a sort of locker whose front lets down like a drawbridge to make a kitchen work top, revealing shelves on which food and saucepans are stacked. Under this is a clothes cupboard. Opposite it is a four-foot bench called by narrow-boat folk a bunk. At the far end is the bed, five foot six inches by three feet, hung with lace curtains. Beyond the bed is a partition, and beyond the partition is the engine, which presumably served to keep the bed warm. A boatman, his wife, and their children would all have lived in a cabin this size. A well-swung cat would have its skull fractured before it could ring the RSPCA.

All the metal except the stove is brass, kept in a mirror-like state of polish. All the visible wood is artificially grained with paint and a brush. The only light comes in through two small circular portholes, one on either side of the cabin, curtained by little lace doilies. Flat surfaces such as the panels of the dresser and the doors are painted with wreaths of roses or with a variation on a theme of castles, a drawbridge, mountains and the sea or a river. Nobody seems to know the origin of this pattern. My own theory is that it is the product of man's desire to see something steep when looking at flat stuff. In the same way, the denizens of the high Andes probably contemplate pictures of billiard tables.

There is a public house in Long Itchington famous for its malt whiskies. They were not the only spirits in the place; it was also apparently haunted. We went there and tried some Laphroaig, and spoke of ghosts in general. Ginny said that one of the tunnels on the Grand Union was haunted. A narrow-boat man was chugging though one day, towing a boat on which his wife was cooking them breakfast. The wife, a terrible scold, was nagging him about something or other. In the middle of the tunnel the husband became so incensed that he cut the towrope. The wife was run down by the next boat through and drowned. Ever since, the tunnel has reeked of bacon and eggs.

This terrifying narrative resulted in the barman's being summoned again. He was a toad-like Glaswegian, with what appeared to be a suspicious mind. Earlier in the evening he had delighted us by recounting a long story whose punchline was that some unscrupulous villain had robbed him of eight and a half pence by mistiming a telephone call. Now I asked him about the ghost in the pub.

'Him?' he said. 'If I meet the bugger I'll kill him.'

I would never make a bargee. This I realized the following morning, when I awoke from a fitful slumber looking like half an SS insignia. There is a very pronounced dark side to narrow-boating.

Martin, the carpenter who had helped repair *Magdalen*, discovered this during his first interview with a narrow boat. He said that while he did not expect white ducks and yachting caps, he had been ready for a paintbrush, a spot of real ale and some rough good-fellowship. It was a bit of a shock, he said, to be put in the hold of the narrow boat in question with a pickaxe and instructions to chip away the cement that the craft had spent its working life carrying. Nor, he says, were his troubles over at the conclusion of the pickaxe job, because the day after he finished that he turned up to find his taskmasters feeding a fire under an oil drum in which bubbled a black mixture with a smell that was knocking racing pigeons out of the sky at a range of two hundred feet. This was the caulking compound, and its ingredients were tar and horse dung. Soon afterwards, he made his excuses and left.

At breakfast Ginny asked if I had slept well. Of course I said yes. She said that was good, because the only problem with canals as far as she was concerned was the arthritis. She already had arthritis in her right knee, she said, and did not know if this was normal at the age of twenty-three. She suspected it was not.

On the last flight of locks before Napton Junction brought to my appointment with Destiny on the Oxford Canal, I met a lock-keeper with a Flymo. He had walked three miles with his Flymo. According to my calculations he had another sixty miles to walk, to and fro, to and fro, before he was finished. We conversed of this and that. He was looking embarrassed; I could not think why. His embarrassment deepened until he was bright red and shifting from foot to foot. Finally, he asked me if I had a licence. I said yes, and asked him if he wanted to see it. No, no, no, he said, hastily. Not a bit.

'Why didn't you ask me for it straight out?' I asked.

His face crumpled slightly at the edges. 'I . . . well, people you get through here in the summer . . . that is, I was afraid you might tell me to f— off.' When I asked him about the Oxford Canal, he did not know. But he said it was more than likely.

Two hours later, I arrived at a T-junction. To the left lay Rugby and the North. To the right was Oxford and the Thames. If there was any water to row on.

As Napton Hill rose on the left, our progress became furtive. I steered under the bank, hoping that British Waterways Board personnel would not notice. At the first lock, a man was leaning against the wall watching the canal. I cleared my throat, marshalled my arguments and stepped ashore.

'I have to get through your lock,' I said. 'I am delivering this boat to a dear friend in Cropredy, who will be tremendously disappointed if he does not get it on his birthday, which happens to be tomorrow.'

The man looked me up and down. His eyes were blue and watery. 'Well, well,' he said, eventually. 'Really, now? Lock's open.'

'So it's all right?' I said, with a rush of relief. 'That's very good of you, My – er – friend will be delighted.'

'Don't thank me,' said the man. 'I've just come to read the electric in the lock cottage.'

CHAPTER EIGHT

Napton to Duke's Cut

*Uphill with dysentery – A vanished village and where it went – A gale
and our future Queen – A technical full stop – Foolish giggling –
Soundings in the canal – The Banbury spellers – A new Beaufort scale –
Lords of creation in hire boats – A one-man temporary soaking-wet peace
camp – Enter the green narrow boat – Still waters run out*

The Oxford Canal travels up to the roof of the world via Napton Locks. You start in a deep valley; slowly, you travel upwards until you are on the same level as the windmill on Napton Hill. Being by now entirely fed up with locks, the sign NAPTON BOTTOM LOCK gave me an unpleasant sinking feeling. This sinking feeling grew more pronounced. By the top, it had metamorphosed into an attack of dysentery. The only book in my possession which had any bearing on this disease was *The Happy Traveller*, by Frank Tatchell, Vicar of Midhurst around 1927. He advises the traveller to take salol tablets in a little whisky, and chlorodyne.' If you catch it in the wilds and have no drugs,' continues Revd Tatchell, 'chew wood charcoal or scrape a powder from a charred stick and swallow it with water.' My first-aid kit did not contain any salol tables, nor indeed chlorodyne or burnt sticks. There was, however, a small dose of whisky. This I followed with a carefully selected invalid's luncheon of cheese, pickled onions, false bread, and margarine. I then continued up the locks, bent double and sweating profusely.

At the top a narrow boat came past and I hitched a lift. By now it was teatime. We spoke of this and that, mainly the beauties of the St Albans – Watford area. They offered me cake, which I accepted. It was the fruit model, about the same density as gold. Soon afterwards I made my excuses, leaped for the bank, and knew no more for some twenty minutes. On my return to the world, the narrow boat was far ahead.

The Oxford Canal is another of Brindley's efforts, and reflects his dislike for installing any more locks than he absolutely had to. Between Marston Doles and Claydon, the cut winds round the hills for nine miles, following the contours. It moves on the same level as the clouds. That evening, the late sun poured a syrupy, greenish light over the woods and meadows and farms until it looked good enough to eat, even if you had dysentery. I camped in gathering darkness near Wormleighton, and ate a medicinal dinner of plain boiled rice.

Wormleighton is a clump of Victorian buildings near a church in the middle of a sea of black ploughland into which tractors were drilling winter barley. They drilled all night, engines roaring and headlamps splashing sheets of white light across the hummocky ground on the far side of the canal; the hummocky ground that was the old Wormleighton.

In the thirteenth century Wormleighton had a thatched manor house and forty homesteads. Three hundred years later it had none. This had little to do with the Black Death, or rural drift or urban seep. It was because there was a wool boom on, and the sheep ranchers were buying up the farms and there was no room for homesteads any more. So Wormleighton passed into the hands of John Spencer, a grazier. And he built himself a manor house and became Sir John, and the grass grew over the ruins of the homesteads and was grazed by the sheep that were making him rich.

And five hundred years later, the Spencers, earls by now, built a new village. The earl who put it up was a Victorian of the sterner type, so there is a large village hall, but no public house. And the land is still in Spencer hands. The exigencies of taxation and the difficulty of having tenant farmers (you might as well give your land away as let it) have led to a new system, with very much the same effect as the old. It is called share or partnership farming because a landowner goes into partnership with a farmer, and the farmer does the work, while the landowner provides the land. The money they make is split between them in an agreed proportion. If the farmer had been a tenant, the rent would have been unearned income for the landlord, subject to a fifteen per cent tax surcharge. But since the landlord is a partner in the farm, the income is earned, and there is no surcharge. Also, if he wishes to dissolve the partnership he can do so, and the farmer is off camping in a lay-by with his potato machinery . . .

Of course, this never happens. Well, almost never. What does happen is that young people trying to get into farming find that there are fewer farms needing tenants than before (when there were few enough in all conscience), that landowners are pretty reluctant to go into partnership with people straight out of agricultural college, and that young farmers have spent three years of their lives educating themselves for a tied cottage on someone else's farm, if they are lucky, or the dole queue, if they are not.

History tends to repeat itself at Wormleighton.

On a contour canal there is a tendency for the voyager to travel two miles north, east and west in order to proceed one mile south. Under normal circumstances this is irritating. On my first Oxford Canal morning, however, it was extremely handy. The weather forecast had predicted southerly gales, so one naturally expected a light wind from the north. To my horror the southerly gales commenced, blowing force eight to nine. They had little effect at the beginning, since the canal wove round the sides of several hills, and never made up its mind to pursue any course for more than a hundred yards.

But shortly after I had respectfully taken off my hat to the end of a manor house which presumably once resounded to the merriment of Lady Di's forebears, I rounded a corner, the wind hit me in the back of the neck like an articulated lorry, and that was more or less that.

Magdalen is not a boat that enjoys forward progress, preferring, as I have already pointed out, to indulge in the wallow to port and the obstructive settle. The Wormleighton wind bent willows parallel to the ground. It shrieked in the thorn bushes and howled in the barbed-wire fences. The water of the canal rose in an eighteen-inch swell whose tops were torn to spindrift. *Magdalen* rocked violently, wallowed and settled. I hacked at the water with my oars to keep her bow straight, holding my ground with difficulty. It was then that she demonstrated a new manoeuvre, the sideways wamble. In the sideways wamble, *Magdalen* suggests that the only way forward is to zig and zag as if tacking under sail. The rower accordingly makes like a convoy in the Battle of the Atlantic, and is pleased to see a wake develop, and hear the chuckle of a bow wave under the boat's nose. This continues for ten minutes, after which he checks landmarks on the bank, and discovers that the five hundred strokes he has just rowed have resulted in forward progress of 3.25 inches. At this point he struggles to the towpath, gets out the rope, attaches it to the boat and begins dragging it towards Oxford. Rowing, in these circumstances, is a waste of time.

It was here that I met for the first time on the journey a technical full stop. By this I mean an obstacle that demolishes the illusion of progress and restores a sense of scale, thereby giving rise to thoughts of abandon-ship-and-pass-the-cyanide-capsule.

In this case it was a thorn bush, three feet high, three feet wide, and three feet deep; one cubic yard of air, densely laced with spines. I had been using it as a bank mark while trying to row. Now I had come ashore, twenty yards downwind of the bush, with the intention of towing. Rigging up a bridle (a towline with one end attached to bow and the other to stern), I dragged *Magdalen* in the desired direction. The bush intervened. I flipped the towrope over it. The wind caught the rope in mid-flip, weaving it among the branches and spines. I pulled. It would not disengage. Instead *Magdalen* plunged her stupid head into the bush and stuck. I hurled myself into the middle of it, blackthorns running deep into hand, and untied the bow line, pushing off by the head. She swung away. The wind caught her, and she drifted back the way she had come until the stern line caught. Then she came alongside the bank and I was able to re-attach the towline and push her off and drag her up to the bush again, with the wind flailing and battering, and flip the rope.

And it happened all over again. Three times. And beyond this bush there stretched an infinite procession of others, and the wind was freshening.

In cases like this, you sit down and smoke a pipe. Gradually the feeling that you will spend the rest of your life trying to get round this particular bush fades. Once again you see it as a mere link in the chain stretching from Plynlimmon to the Houses of Parliament.

Unfortunately I had given up smoking two weeks previously.

So after I had kicked the bush for a bit I took off my trousers, boots and socks and got into the canal and towed *Magdalen* past the bad bit. The canal was icy cold; the waves hit me in the chest and took my breath away. Suddenly I saw myself as if from a helicopter; half–naked, wading in the teeth of an October gale, dragging an overloaded rowing boat. I began to giggle foolishly.

And on we went, and on. After a while, rising ground ahead broke the wind, and I took once again to the oars.

In mid-morning, I stopped at Fenny Compton Marina to get warm and buy some peanuts. The man at the marina was a dedicated head–shaker. While he was shaking his head, he told me that a year ago sixteen Germans had come through in four fast rowing boats, *en route* for Llangollen and York, starting-point London. They were beautifully organized, he said, nervously eyeing the battered and flapping *Magdalen*. Their chief complaint as rowers was that the motor boats would not get out of their way. I must have looked shaken, because he gave me a cup of coffee. Then I set off again.

After an interval of shelter in the deep cutting that used to be Fenny Compton Tunnel, the wind returned. *Magdalen* began to prove that the wallow to port was not a manoeuvre reserved for towing. In addition, alarming things were happening to my hands, now huge and blue and extremely dirty, with little cynical laughter lines spreading from the joints of the fingers, which were locked stiff in the arthritic condor pose already mentioned. On the Fenny Compton day, the laughter lines turned into little crevasses, yawning down to the attractive pink base-level. This was extremely painful.

At Claydon Locks, the Oxford Canal starts heading downhill towards the valley of the Cherwell. This should have been encouraging. At the first lock, however, the pain of manipulating the windlass was so extreme that while raising a paddle I managed to let go of it. The paddle went down with a hideous rattle and the windlass disappeared, rather as a Sopwith Camel's airscrew disappears when you start the engine. There was a *ping* and a crash, and a violent pain in the right arm.

As I folded over said arm I caught sight of the windlass. It was describing an attractive arc in the sky. The arc terminated in a small splash in the exact centre of the canal, where there was probably eight feet of water. A red mist covered my eyes and I slumped to the ground, grunting. It was the only windlass I had. Also, I suspected my arm was broken, but that was not significant. You can get down the Oxford with one arm, but not without a windlass.

For a while I could not move the fingers. Hospital job, I thought. But after a bit I could move them fine; it was just that I couldn't feel them. As oarsmen know, the correct countermove to wallow to port is a good jab at the water with the right oar. Now, this more often than not resulted in the loss of the oar. The only bright spot was that I realized I could open locks with my mole wrench, in only four times as long as it took with the windlass.

The wind continuing unabated, I thought the best thing to do was tow as far as possible, while the arm renewed itself. Accordingly, I commenced yomping down the towpath, which for a change was bushless.

Towpaths were once the backbone of the canal system. But since the invention of the internal combustion engine they have fallen on hard times. They were originally intended for horses; the British Waterways Board, with the concern for history which typifies its every move and gesture, has recently issued a proclamation banning horses from all towpaths unless they happen to be bridleways as well. Not that anyone in their right mind would take a horse down the towpath of the Oxford Canal, unless they wished to drown it after first stunning it. Towpath maintenance is low priority stuff, so those parts which have not already collapsed into the water are usually covered with a layer of greasy mud.

Picture, if you will, the voyager. The gale plucks at his wet waterproof garments. The hands with which he is dragging the now chipped and scarred boat drip blood from many fissures. His hair, the colour of mouldy hay, hangs in his lacklustre eyes. The five-day beard grubbing up his face is matted with clots of food residues, among which can be seen patches of bare blue skin. His step is faltering. Wearily, he leaps yet another yawning gulf in the towpath. A lock is in sight. His pace quickens. His gumboot hits a shiny patch. His feet shoot from under him.

He falls into the bleeding canal, right . . . up . . . to . . . the . . . neck.

Oddly, as he crawls out he is laughing. There is something unhealthy about the laughter. A hire boat is coming up the lock, and its comely female occupant greets him with a cheery 'Good day!' He tell the lady occupant of his desire to perform natural functions in the canal, and then to force the chairman of the BWB to drink it all, and subsequently to dynamite the locks.

It comes on to rain, like fire hoses. He opens the next four locks with a mole wrench. Night falls; he camps near a sewage farm, whimpering with agony.

He sleeps.

Banbury is famous for its cakes, as everyone knows. What is less well known is that the spelling of the Banbury area is among the most fascinating in England. Howard Williams, a somewhat priggish cove who undertook a rowing tour from Oxford to London (via Warwick, Gloucester, Hereford and Bristol) in 1875, saw a notice near here that read as follows:

HAY, CORN, BRED
AND COLES
SOLDE HEAR

S. Llewellyn, passing through Banbury on a consummately foul morning in 1982, was privileged to witness the follow notice: DANGER CORROSIVE CHEMCIALS. No, sorry, that was where he camped the previous night. NO MOORING HEAR, said the notice. It was hard to be sure whether it was the spelling or the punctuation that was wrong.

Magdalen's fame seemed to have spread down the canal. Next morning we were given a cup of tea by a lady who lived in a lock-keeper's cottage. When she heard about my windlass she gave me one of hers. She was a spinner. She spun everything from hessian to silk and she had a wonderful garden in which various kinds of vegetables came leaping out of the turf at unpredictable intervals round the lock. Sue was kind and charming, and three hundred years ago someone would have burned her as a witch. Further down, another lady gave me another cup of tea, and chatted. She lived a long way from the road, but she had a tugboat moored in the pound, and every couple of weeks she nipped up to Banbury to do the shopping. We discussed the story of her recent life in some detail. While I was there the telephone rang. She talked for some time, then turned round and said that was a bloke she used to go out with. He was fine. I said I was glad to hear it. Yes, she said, he came and ast me to marry him a bit ago; I knew he had a girlfriend. I didn't want much to do with him, so I said no, and three months later the girlfriend had a baby – his – and now they're getting married. Funny thing, life.

I said it was. When I went out of the door the wind nearly knocked me down.

The Beaufort scale has been revised for use on the Oxford Canal.

Force	Signs	Speed (knots)
0 Calm	Total darkness with smell of sardines. You are probably in a tunnel.	1
1 Light air	The smell of sardines is still engulfing you. Keep a wet handkerchief to the nostrils.	1–3
2 Light breeze	Smell of sardines lessens. Smell of sewage works on windward bank prevalent.	4–6
3 Gentle breeze	Ripples on water. Foreign objects drift towards you from sewage works on windward bank.	7–10

Force	Signs	Speed (knots)
4 Moderate breeze	Map blows into canal. Cursing still audible.	11–16
5 Fresh breeze	Curses torn from lips. Map sunk by waves.	17–21
6 Strong breeze	Howling in ears. Hands hurt. Fishermen in homicidal frame of mind. Wallow to port constant.	22–27
7 Near gale	This and higher numbers invariably blow from the direction in which you are heading. Tent flaps uncontrollably. Sideways wamble evident.	28–33
8 Gale	Sideways wamble becomes backwards wamble. Iron lung movements from tent produce involuntary breathing. Danger of suffocation.	34–40
9 Strong gale	Coffee blown into gumboot instead of cup. Towing possible only on all fours with line between teeth.	41–47
10 Storm	Whole tent in motion. Oak trees behave like butterflies.	48–55
11 Violent storm	Very rarely experienced inland except on the Oxford Canal: severe damage to just about everything.	56–63
12 Hurricane	Very rarely experienced inland even on the Oxford Canal, except south of Banbury on Sunday mornings. May signify end of world imminent.	64+

High winds do peculiar things to human behaviour. (I will leave my own out of the reckoning for the moment, since exhaustion and exposure had already twisted it beyond recognition.) It was made even more peculiar because the day was a Sunday, and it is on Saturdays and Sundays that hire boats change hands, and people who have never driven anything bigger than a Mini Metro suddenly find themselves at the helm of a seventy-foot narrow boat.

The wind was blowing from the south, extremely hard. Old narrow-boat hands, whistling past at eight knots with a forty-knot tail wind, looked rightly apprehensive. The new entries were distinguishable by their general air of being lords of creation, and the lofty disdain with which they seemed to say that it was for them an everyday matter to enter a seven-foot lock in a seventy-foot boat, travelling sideways.

They also loved to enter bridges sideways, particularly as *Magdalen* was also struggling through. (At bridges the canal narrows to about ten feet, and the wind funnels through at up to sixty knots. The rower starts with shortened oars but invariably has recourse to teeth and nails in the final inches.)

There were many plucky attempts to enter locks in which I was descending by ramming the lower gates. But the preferred method was the simple crush lateral. In this, the hire boat waits till the rowing boat is abreast, and then runs aground by the stern, so positioning itself on the wind that its bow is blown across like a huge steel flail, accompanied by the distant screaming of insurance companies.

Upper Heyford is a charming spot. I arrived near it as night was falling, and pitched the tent in a green meadow. It had been an unpleasant day; I was still shuddering with remembered terror, and after nine hours of ceaseless striving, Banbury lay a mere ten miles behind. The ground seemed moistish, but I was too tired to worry about that. The tent went on the driest bit of it. I stumbled through the familiar evening rituals: boil water on stove, cook rice, drop envelope of stew into the water, wait for seven minutes: extract stew and rice, burn fingers, devour food, wash face in water, write diary. Halfway through the diary operation I fell asleep.

Much later I woke up in pitch darkness with my finely tuned senses administering alarm signals, and reached out on to the groundsheet for the matches. My hand touched water, in which individual matches seemed to be floating. This was an unpleasant blow, but by no means fatal; with the foresight of the true woodsman I was sleeping in my trousers, in whose pocket I had left another box of matches. With these I lit the lamp.

The tent was flooded to a depth of two inches. This was extremely interesting, but my camp-bed supported me two and a quarter inches off the ground and I would therefore be able to sleep on, unless the floods rose. Most of my gear was soaked. I did not care. Rolling over, I nodded off again.

I was sitting in a deck chair at the base of a six-hundred-foot cliff. Someone had just dynamited the whole works. I knew this because I had heard the explosion. It had started as a dull rumble, and was now so loud that my ears hurt. High above, among wheeling clouds of terrified gulls, giant slabs of black basalt were shuffling themselves like packs of cards, prior to hurtling into my gin and tonic.

I awoke with a start. The noise was so loud it made my teeth ache. Creeping out of the tent into the freezing dawn, I observed that along the crest of the hill to the east there ran a long line of wire netting, topped with barbed wire. A few feet above this, an aeroplane was approaching at about 200 m.p.h. At it passed overhead, I could have counted the rivets on its belly had I not been face down in the flooded meadow with my hands over my ears. As I picked myself up and spat out the mud, I realized that I was a one-man temporary soaking-wet peace camp.

The end of the Upper Heyford USAF main runway is not, I would like to assure the prospective camper, the ideal spot for the overnight stop, because they keep F1-11s there to carry their hydrogen bombs around. Wringing out my gear, I set off. Upper Heyford had fixed it. No more canals, after today. I was sick of the bloody things. Today it was Oxford or bust.

The lower part of the Oxford Canal is stunningly beautiful, and the weather decided to match it. At Heyford Locks, a lovely rifle-brigade-green narrow boat plumed blue smoke from a gilded chimney and spread the smell of bacon and eggs over the water. A sharp frost had picked out every twig in white rime, and given the banks an edge of ice that jingled very faintly in *Magdalen*'s wake. Oak trees overhanging the cut bombarded the water with acorns; sycamore seeds helicoptered down from steep hillsides matted with old man's beard. Moorhens scuttled around in their usual state of high indignation. As I ate a breakfast of digestive biscuits and margarine, a roach flapped by with a bite-shaped hole where its tail should have been. The seat was very hard this morning; I knew how that fish felt. Groaning, I pulled on into a country of cut stone bridges and locks that somehow contrived to be beautiful. The green narrow boat overtook; its crew told me it was a lovely morning, and there was nothing for it but to agree.

The gales had gone, and *Magdalen* cut the water like a fat scythe. I overtook the green narrow boat again. My thoughts turned to the mighty Thames, and the joy of proceeding along a waterway with the assistance of a current. I was miles away, bowling past Hampton Court with a glass of champagne in my hand, as I came up to Gibraltar Lock. A final stroke of the oars, and I rose to my feet prior to stepping ashore as I had done perhaps a hundred and sixty times since Worcester. As I raised my foot, *Magdalen* made a curious movement that started as a shimmy and developed into a full-scale wallow to port, executed at lightning speed. My feet shot across the canal, leaving my body behind. The back of my head hit the concrete coping, and my feet remained hooked over the gunwale. Constellations of brilliant stars swam before my eyes. Despite the unwelcome sensations induced by a violent blow to the skull, one thing was clear. Llewellyn was now a human mooring line, and if he was to stay dry should maintain the hawser imitation for as long as possible. Despite a curious flickering in the mind, I was able to keep myself rigid for fifteen seconds or so. After that, muscular strain began to take effect, and I folded like a penknife, screaming shrilly as the water (which was at ideal Martini temperature) penetrated the inner garments. I swam ashore, recaptured the boat and looked about. The green narrow boat had seeped up behind me. A charming lady was standing in the bows, wrestling with something in a small black case.

'Do you think,' she said, 'you could possibly do that again? Only my camera case zipper's stuck.'

In the early evening I passed through Duke's Lock. Below it, Duke's Cut runs off to the right. A sign pointing the way I had come said MIDLANDS. Shaking the dust of the towpath from my feet, I pulled along the backwater and out into the broad, glittering Thames.

Amazingly, an inch of whisky remained in the half-bottle I had brought from Llanidloes. I drank it, pouring the last drips as a libation into the flood. We were fifteen days out from Plynlimmon. We had covered more than two hundred and thirty miles of rapids and pools and stagnant water and locks. From now on, the locks would have keepers. We were back in the cradle of civilization. Surely *this* time we were on the finishing straight?

But after my recent experience of the rewards of cockiness, I kept my mouth shut.

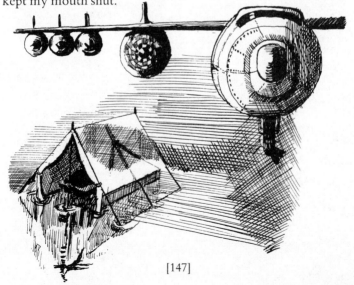

Part Three

CHAPTER NINE

Duke's Cut to Clifton Hampden

*Duke's Cut – The reputation of the fashionable Thames – Fair
Rosamund's odour – Bottles for two, stomach pumps for one –
Magdalen's sullenness – Sightseeing on the Thames – Pecking about on
the river – Death of a public house – The fiend in the boathouse –
Health note.*

Duke's Cut threads between tree-clad islands. Its smooth surface was covered in leaves – spearhead willow, yellow beech,
fire-brown chestnut, and jaundiced sycamore. After the canals,
the backwater seemed to ride very high in its banks, contained by
nothing more than an inch or two of silt. We kept to the northern
side; Duke's Cut joins the main river just above King's Weir, and
I had heard dire tales of the Thames weir streams. But when we
joined the main stream, I forgot about weirs and leaned on the
oars and drifted, with my mouth open.

Twenty minutes ago, we had been flogging along a ditch of
dirty water flanked by allotments and run-down housing estates.
Now the cut spilled us on to a broad stripe of jade between fringes
of bulrush as lush as sugar cane, from which an elephant or a
brontosaurus might at any point appear. I sat and stared, and tried
to make a link with that brawling ribbon of gin-coloured water
among the hills at Llanidloes.

These reflections were interrupted by the realization that we
were now in the mainstream current, and being swept at speed
towards a line of white posts with fluorescent stripes, bearing a
large sign that said DANGER. I began pulling away in the direction
of the lock.

The Thames is divided into two parts, the fashionable bit and the
unfashionable bit. At King's Lock and above, it is unfashionable;
the paddles of the locks are worked by hand, and the lock-
keepers, though spruce enough for a royal inspection, carry with
them a faint whiff of manual toil. Below King's Lock, the locks
are worked by hydraulics, and their keepers have a general air of

being lords of all they survey. This is the territory of the parasol and the punt, the rowing eight and the boater-ribbon, the pink gin and the slipper launch. The river is managed and cosseted, improved and denatured, and the lock-keepers work hard at taming it. But it tends to burst through. It is on the fashionable part of the Thames that much of its reputation is based.

The reputation of the fashionable Thames (because by this time I was through King's Lock, drifting across Port Meadow, and night was falling) is severe. Its currents are spoken of in hushed tones, as running in the vertical as well as in the horizontal plane. Human bodies caught in the eddies of the weir pools are found months later, miles downstream, horribly mangled. Its weirs crop up in peculiar places, lurking in clumps of bushes and on the approaches to locks, where on any other river there would be a bank. Its navigators are not restricted by the 4 m.p.h. limit that saves the canal fiend from injury; on the Thames it is 6 m.p.h. upstream and 8 m.p.h. downstream, and the boats that travel at this huge speed are fibreglass juggernauts, miles high and yards wide, with, at their helms, timid lathe-minders from Galashiels, Donald Campbells one and all, with the throttles under their palms . . .

Everyone said you have to be careful on the Thames.

Below King's Lock, the river begins the restless splitting into sidestreams and backwaters that makes the country round Oxford resemble an inland delta. On the right, skeletal walls and towers loomed from the dusk. These were the ruins of Godstow Nunnery, where Fair Rosamund lies buried. Rosamund had an exciting life, being the mistress of Henry II, and was famous for the dazzling whiteness of her teeth. Like all great beauties, she had tissues of myth woven around her. After her death, they began to fall away when it was discovered that her name was not Rosamund at all, but Jane. She was buried under an insulting Latin epitaph at Godstow.

The epitaph read:

Hic jacet in tumba Rosa mundi, non Rosamunda.

Non redolet, sed olet, quae redolere solet.
Here Rose the chased, not chaste, reposes,
And of corruption stinks, not roses.

As it happened, the writer of the epitaph was wrong. Later, when she was exhumed, it was found that she had been buried in a leather bag. When the bag was opened, a delicious scent spread from it. Some say that the bag itself was perfumed; others, that the scent was a supernatural emanation from the bones themselves. The skull in the bag possessed a full set of teeth, of such startling whiteness that the exhumers were amazed, and the myths once again surrounded Rosamund's beauty.

The twentieth-century face of the Thames, or Isis, as it is known round these parts, now winked roguishly from the gathering dusk. Runners puffed down the towpath. As the lights started to go on in distant houses I tied up at the jetty opposite one of the pubs which has made Oxford famous: the Perch. The open window of a cabin cruiser was releasing a stream of drunken cursing on to the night air, and as I padlocked *Magdalen* to the leg of the jetty, I worked out that the cursing was coming from two throats, one male, one female. The female was unquestionably far gone in the juice. The male also; except that when he heard me tying up, he came out (leaving Herself making dreadful thuddings in the hull) and saluted me courteously from the lofty altitudes of his cleft palate. Leaving *Magdalen* under his protection, I scurried into Oxford to stay with friends.

Next morning, I arrived back at the jetty filled with apprehension. This was partly what psychologists call a mood thing, since it had been my task that morning to persuade Matthew, aged five, to drink his nice worm medicine before breakfast. This he had quite reasonably refused to do until I had sketched the effect of bilharzia on the human eyeball, and (more effectively) bribed him with 20p for Smarties. I therefore arrived at the jetty with my mind full of diagrams of the human digestive tract. *Magdalen* was still there, as was the cabin cruiser. From the bowels of the latter there came awful screechings, interspersed with dire thuds and the sounds of pumping. *Magdalen* was tugging at the painter. It was none of our business. Besides, the windows were steamed up. Silently, I unpadlocked and drifted away with the stream.

The Oxford ring road rises above the plain on its embankment like a medieval city wall. On a slab of concrete near the bank, an unseen but highly educated hand had written in red aerosol: MELISSA IS A SLUT.

In Osney Lock, I met up with the rifle-brigade-green narrow boat once again. We introduced ourselves; they were Mr and Mrs Smail, heading for London. They offered me a tow. Laughing lightly and waving a hand at the wondrous clarity of the sky, I said I didn't think there would be any need for that sort of thing. The Smails looked doubtful but polite. Possibly they were remembering the human mooring rope on the Oxford Canal. Outside the lock we parted.

At Folly Bridge I tied up to a raft and went into the town and bought maps, lardy cake and steak and kidney pies. The latter are obtainable at the pie shop in Oxford Market, and are the best in England.

Down by Folly Bridge a beautiful blonde woman was scrubbing out an Elsan with a kitchen brush. I told her she looked flushed, upon which she smiled, showing keen intelligence and a highly evolved sense of humour, and asked me into her houseboat for a cup of tea. There, under the doe-eyed gaze of the Dinka women in the photographs on the walls, she introduced me to her boyfriend. For an hour or so we planned an assault on the Tana river in Kenya, to be undertaken next year in the light of experience hard won on the Worcester and Birmingham Canal. Then I climbed back into *Magdalen* and set off downstream.

Below Christ Church Meadow the college barges lie. Some of them are crisp, upright craft, well used to the swarms of pleasure seekers who invade them each summer during Eights' week. Others are derelict and peeling, stuffed up backwaters with their barley-sugar columns and oriel windows and baroque balustrading collapsing into the river. As we passed, I realized that many of these hulks were in fact only half *Magdalen*'s age; and *Magdalen* read my mind.

Perhaps she was already a little demoralized by the Thames. On the Severn and the canals, she had tended to be rather snooty about the boats she met. On the Thames, she had expected to be among equals. But since Folly Bridge, she had realized that she was merely a small rowing boat with a lot of paint rubbed off her; and the *scale* of the college barges, the fact that even in decay they were six times the boat she would ever be, depressed her badly.

In vain I told her that college barges were foolish, static things, whereas she had served in the nine oceans and had even now travelled two hundred and fifty miles, some of them uncharted. Finally I was forced to be sharp with her. I told her that if we did not reach London I would not be able to hold my head up in society, and nor would she. She said it was all right for me, but did I realize that she was eighty-three years old and frail with it? Soothingly I replied yes, I did, but that she must not give up, particularly because it was by no means off the cards that I would give her there and then a deadly skelp of the boot and hire one of those nice sharp plastic boats below at the dock. She capitulated. We pushed off again.

During the next hour, the wind rose steadily. It blew south to north. My course lay from north to south. It blew and blew, and then blew some more. The world condensed into a little hemisphere of grey rain and slapping waves and pain from cracked hands. A boat was coming up astern. Mr and Mrs Smail, in the rifle-brigade-green narrow boat. Cheerily, they waved a towrope. I climbed aboard.

The banks slid by. The rain came down. The fifty-horsepower Mercedes diesel throbbed underfoot. *Magdalen* trailed behind, looking small and sorry for herself.

Sightseeing on the Thames is a source of constant difficulty. Being British, the ambition of the Thames helmsman is to get along as fast as possible, looking neither to right nor left, blowing bugles and horns to ginger up the lock-keepers, and cursing constantly when prevented from overtaking. Unfortunately, the helmsman usually has passengers in his boat. The passengers are quite oblivious of the skill and experience being displayed by the helmsman. As he roars past Abingdon with the rev counter jammed on its pin and the plates vibrating off the galley shelves, the passengers make mouthings. Their yells come as a sort of distant hissing above the thunder of the diesels. They wish, it appears, to view the almshouses for which Abingdon is noted. The intelligent helmsman taps the throttle up a couple of notches and roars, 'WHAT?'

'WE WANT TO GO AND LOOK AT THE ALMSHOUSES!' yell the aesthetes.

'SORRY? LOOK OUT!' Here the helmsman executes a tight S-curve to avoid an imaginary obstacle in the river, unbalancing the aesthetes, who are rendered speechless by fear and cling, gibbering, to the rail on the cabin top. Now is the time for the helmsman to press home his advantage. As the final houses of Abingdon flash by he throttles back and says to the whitest aesthete, 'You all right, old thing? Look all shaken up. Thought we might stop in Wallingford. Lovely place.'

'Almshouses . . .' whimpers the aesthete.

'Oh, them? Didn't you see 'em? I went specially close to the bank. You get a sort of glimpse of 'em by those iron railings, but you have to be quick. Well, Wallingford, here we come!'

And by the time you get to Wallingford, it is dark, and after opening time, and you are safe.

The Smails' narrow boat was called *Dyfed* and was extremely luxurious, with a large saloon, a bathroom, two bedrooms and a galley with hot running water. Bingo Smail, the boss, explained that he and Dilys had decided to buy it instead of a weekend cottage. There were a good few weekenders on the canals; in addition, there were other categories of folk. At the bottom of this pyramid were the hire people. Above them came the gypsies, chugging round in rotting hulks emitting clouds of scarcely digested diesel. Above these came the rally folk, similar to caravan fiends, who drove short (forty-foot) boats done up to the nines and went to rallies in order to discuss the next rally they were going to. Above these came the purists in their work boats, as found at Long Itchington. And above the lot came the inhabitants of *Dyfed* and similar. I put it to him that above them all came rowing boats with adventurous pasts, such as *Magdalen*. He smiled tolerantly and changed the subject.

There was one other category, occurring (in the estimation of the Smails) so far down in the pyramid as to resemble the king's chamber of Cheops. This was the noddy boat, or gigantic fibreglass wedding cake, whose habitat was the Thames. Noddy boats were by definition unable to enter a lock, except sideways or backwards; unable to tie up, except in the strongest part of the current, using a combination of slippery hitches and knitting wool, and were as lethal as psychotic cruise missiles. I laughed and shook my head. Later, I was to discover that noddy-boat folk have prejudices of their own.

The Smails dropped me at Clifton Cut, in a rainstorm. They were stopping for the night, and strongly suggested that I did too. They would tow me down to London, they said. No, no, I replied; thing worth doing worth doing properly, press on regardless, as well hung for sheep as lamb. I pulled briskly into the rain. Water sloshed around my feet: *Magdalen* had decided to start leaking again.

It was my intention to write at length about the scenic beauties of the Thames. Unfortunately these had retired behind the rainstorm. Soon I passed under a bridge and perceived a grassy bank on the right. Here I landed, unloaded, and erected tent. Everything in the container seemed suspiciously wet. When I emptied it, I found in the bottom one wet sock, which had been fulfilling the function of the bit of orange peel in the tin of tobacco. I looped string across the inside of the tent, suspended all my possessions from it, and turned up the cooking stove full blast. Then I retreated into the rain, bearing a large sheet of polythene, which I draped over *Magdalen*. She had been leaking solidly, and with consistency. Examination of her port side showed that where the copper plate had been there were three or four loose rivets, which had been moving about, wearing the timbers into holes that admitted a constant stream of water. So I slapped on some more plastic padding (the sixth tube, large size) left the polythene in place, and decided to go to the pub and sit near the fire. I was camped at Clifton Hampden, home of the Barley Mow, as mentioned in *Three Men in a Boat*. Jerome K. Jerome say that it is 'without exception the quaintest, most old-world inn on the river', and observes that tall ladies given to drawing themselves up to their full heights will bump their heads on the low ceilings. Surveys show that where there are low ceilings there are usually nice log fires.

Perhaps it would have been better for the Barley Mow if Jerome had not mentioned it, because literary fame seems to have gone to its head. It is now owned by Grand Metropolitan Hotels, who have done a job on it. If they owned a pub once frequented by Ernest Hemingway it would probably have a *For Whom the Bell Tolls* Bar, and a *Death in the Afternoon* Lounge in which *Old Man and the Sea* Lunches (soaked mackerel in a basket) would be served. As it is, the Barley Mow has bedrooms called J., George, Harris and Montmorency, and a menu which, though probably delicious, bears main dishes named after the same cast of characters.

Nobody in the public bar banged her head on the beams, though it is fair to say that some of the gentlemen round the local's table looked about ready to bang theirs on the floor. One of them, who resembled Mahatma Gandhi, poured pints of whisky mac through a new set of false teeth, and spoke of his cat, which could make mincemeat of a dachshund and a fricassee out of a fox. He sounded as if he might produce this monster, so I left.

Outside, the rain was falling in horizontal sheets, and the tent flapped like M. Bleriot's monoplane in mid-takeoff. I crept into two wet sleeping bags, listened to the weatherman forecasting low-pressure areas with associated fronts, laughed heartily and became unconscious.

What I did not know at the time was that earlier in the year the Mexican volcano El Chichon (the Lump) had erupted, squirting vast quantities of dust into the stratosphere and providing almost unlimited quantities of what meteorologists call nuclei of condensation for raindrops. The dust clouds had, unknown to me, reached the Thames Valley at the same time as self and *Magdalen*. At eight a.m. on 21 October, the rain was coming down on the tent with a relentless drumming, driven by a forty-mile-an-hour south wind.

In the literature of the Thames it is traditional at this point to turn to one's travelling companion and suggest diffidently that the sensible thing to do is to ring up a waterman and have him take the boat home for you while you hop on a train for London and get something hot to eat and the valet brings some dry clothes from the country in the two-seater. This seemed a sensible idea. There were, however, obstacles, the worst of which was that I had no companion but *Magdalen*, with whom I was no longer on speaking terms, and my conscience, which urged me to continue downriver. Wetly, I caved in; the ghosts of Jerome K. Jerome and J. C. Squire jeered audibly as I packed *Magdalen* and pushed her into the rain-whipped stream under the dripping gaze of the two limp-wristed lead statues on the terrace of Clifton Hampden Manor.

The sound of Home Counties accents in the Barley Mow the previous night had been heartening. Perhaps too heartening; unwarily, I had slipped into thinking that the journey was all over bar the shouting. It soon became apparent that this was a fallacy.

Half a mile below Clifton Hampden Bridge, the wind was raising a three-foot swell in the centre of the river. (It is unnecessary to point out that the wind was blowing straight upstream.) Once the bridge was out of sight we stuck, in an almost perfect example of the technical full stop. *Magdalen*, newly watertight but still sullen, performed the sideways wamble, the wallow to port and the backwards wamble, all at the same time.

Unfortunately it was not possible to get out and tow, because the vegetation between towpath and bankside on the Thames is tall, and Thames towlines are traditionally attached to a mast to raise them above willow and alder trees. *Magdalen* did not possess a mast. It was obvious that I could not keep up the rowing, and I had no intention of returning to Clifton Hampden; so I slunk in under the bank and hung on to the overhanging branch of a willow tree, which shed pounds of leaves into the boat. From this temporary mooring I was able to take stock.

Just ahead, there was a boathouse. The wind howled up two more octaves, and thirty or forty half-pint raindrops penetrated my ear to the drum. My Shropshire Lad special had given up dripping in favour of continuous running, like a couple of taps. My blue cracked hands were wrinkling on the oar as if left in the bath too long. The boathouse! A promise of shelter, where I could light the stove and make coffee with whisky in it, and while away the worst of the day! *Magdalen*'s nose turned in without my having to apply oar to water. At last, she seemed to say, a bit of common sense.

The garden at The Laurels ran down to the river, where there was a boathouse. It was because of the boathouse that Doktor Karl Petersen and his lovely niece, Irma, had rented The Laurels for the autumn. The boathouse entrance faced north, so it never got the sun: it was as dark as the water lapping at its rotten duckboards.

The white boat carrying the man in the straw hat glided in. A flame flickered under a kettle; the man in the straw hat poured into his steaming cup something from a flat bottle, and drank. After a brief interval of hoarse singing his head slumped on his breast, and he slept. It was late when he awoke with a start, as if disturbed by a sudden sound. 'Is that you, Standish, old man?' he cried, his bloodshot eyes searching the depths of the boathouse. 'I say, Standish, cut rotting, you know, old chap!'

From the depths of the boathouse came a low, inhuman chuckle. Then there was the sound of running bare feet and the slither of calloused knuckles trailing on slimy wood, an agonized cry, cut off suddenly; and the thud of a falling body. 'Come, Igor,' said the voice of a woman, sweet as the tinkling of bells.

Two hours later a periscope glided into the boathouse. A submarine surfaced and a huge, ugly, laughing figure heaved itself through the conning-tower hatch. Algy heard his sharp intake of breath. In the beam of the torch the man in the straw hat lay with his head at a ghastly angle to his body.

'Curse them,' said Hugh Drummond, at length. 'Curse them from Zanzibar to Tartarus and into the Black Pots of Snookerdom. The fiends have struck again!'

While outside in the shadows, a thing with long arms and eyes that were not human gibbered in the top of an elm tree and gnawed at a human finger.

Somehow the boathouse looked unprepossessing. Besides, it was quite early in the morning still, and there was a long way to go. And even if one did travel backwards in midstream, there were always the edges where it was possible to remain stationary, at the same time as taking some violent, health-giving exercise. Yes, we decided, as one. On reflection there was practically nothing that was as much fun as rowing into a force-eight gale during a liquid blizzard.

High in the branches of a wellingtonia, Something that was not human ground its shear-like molars in frustrated rage. 'Later,' said the voice like the tinkling of bells. 'Later, my so-sleek brute, we weel have him. For has he not yet to pass Mapledurham, not to mention Staines?'

The wind abated. Inch by inch, Reading drew nearer. At this rate we would be there by July 1983. Hoorah!

Health note (a consultant writes). It is regrettable to have to report the almost total disintegration of subject's mind and body. While the constant rain had removed some of the blueness from the hands, these appendages were now almost raw and deeply tattooed with grime. The knuckles had swollen to the size of Victoria plums. It was all most distressing.

The bum nerve syndrome had reached an intensity which demanded that much rowing be done kneeling in the bilges facing forward, in order to remove weight from the afflicted part.

The mind seems, from reading diaries constructed at this time, to have been almost completely unhinged. The diaries consist entirely of paranoid fugues: one ten-page section, for instance, explores the possibility that the River Thames is built in a special non-Einsteinian space, given to stretching at unpredictable intervals (with no corresponding effect on the surrounding countryside). Another passage seems to express the view that Didcot power station is following the subject across the fields on huge concrete feet. There are frequent allegations of scale-juggling and other forms of conspiracy and incompetence against HM Ordnance Survey. Interspersed among these are pleas to something, apparently an old woman, to 'stay afloat' – pleas reinforced by bloodcurdling threats involving gasoline and matches. Finally there are 131 versions of the oarsman's last will and testament, many of them illegible. Most of the legible ones leave the testator's piteous possessions to his sons Willie and Martin, on the condition that they never go anywhere near the Thames south or east of Oxford. And at the top of every page, written in characters blurred and smudged by water, are the words, 'Ah, but it is wet! *Wet*! WET!'

CHAPTER TEN

Clifton Hampden to Windsor

Solitude – the attitude of the respectable Thames – Anglers – How to cook a chub – The life, death and resurrection of the grebe – Pangbourne – Muck at Mapledurham – The soup day – Hell's teeth in Cliveden – I flatten a dwarf – Mayhem at Maidenhead – Après moi le deluge – A serious situation – Despair – The green narrow boat

The alert reader will have noticed that human beings have rather faded out of this narrative.

This is partly because battling adverse winds lead to a state of mind in which one half of the oarsman is cursing, pleading with and cajoling the other half to take a few more strokes before he has a rest. This dialogue starts off inside the head, but eventually surfaces as a sort of continuous mumble not calculated to inspire confidence. It is entirely meaningless; behind it, the mind functions with its customary icy clarity. What I knew with icy clarity at this moment was that I wanted to get to London by Sunday. I already knew exactly what I was going to drink: champagne, bottled for the royal wedding by Messrs Bollinger, mingled with draught Guinness. Subsequently I was going to have a bath, with pink bath salts, and a shave with Trumper's soap. Then I was going to sit down in an armchair and read *The Times*, not stopping until I had finished the lot, including the crossword. That evening, Karen and I would dine at an extraordinary restaurant just off Leicester Square . . .

Somehow all this planning left no time for hobnobbing with passers-by. Besides, the stretch of river between Oxford and Windsor is a poor spot for the sociably inclined. The people who do appear seem to have come to the banks either to fish or to nurse a secret sorrow and weigh the pros and cons of self-immolation. Those who are in merrier humour are usually beastly drunk and driving hire cruisers, and are therefore to be a given a wide berth by a creature of *Magdalen*'s high social standards and physical frailty.

At the risk of seeming to harp on an old theme, I have to say that the situation was compounded by the fact that *Magdalen* and self were no oil painting. Lock-keepers treated us with the easy familiarity of dustmen addressing freelance totters. Mostly, the beauty and elegance of the river simply ignored us. This was no skin off my nose, but I could tell it rankled with *Magdalen*, who bears on her transom a brass plaque certifying that she has been swamp-tested at Devonport.

Riparian owners on the Thames operate in a spirit of aggressive mind-your-own-businessry. In the Midlands, a warning notice generally said: DANGER 40,000 VOLTS/TOXIC CHEMICALS/KEEP OFF. Succinct, to the point, and life-threatening. On the Thames, the notices read: NO MOORING / NO CAMPING / NO FISHING / NO BREATHING/PRIVATE/ACT OF PARLIAMENT IN FORCE/TRESPASSERS WILL BE PROSECUTED/THIS MEANS YOU. The implication being that while you will probably get killed if you trespass in the Midlands, on the banks of the Thames you will become involved in litigation that will undoubtedly bankrupt you, as well as being chewed to shreds by Alsatians. (Just after a lock I did see a BEWARE OF ALSATIANS sign. A Great Dane was lifting its leg on it.)

Like all waterways, the Thames is lined with fishermen. They are a special breed, the Thames anglers; they have a tradition that stretches back as far as history. It was the Thames fishermen who pointed out to a king of England that it was not sporting to do his angling with a trained polar bear; the king, realizing he was out of line, sacked the polar bear forthwith. Fishing on the Thames has its own myths and legends. There used to be a waterman at Eton who claimed that a fisherman caught an eel so gigantic (under Windsor Bridge, it was, he remembered it plain as day, yes thank you, his was a pint of Bass) that when it was heaved into the boat it stood on its tail and barked at him, causing him to be terminated with extreme prejudice by Romney Weir.

The dominant fish in this part of the river is the chub, a large creature resembling the carp you see painted on cheap Japanese pottery. Izaak Walton spoke highly of them, as do modern anglers, but for different reasons. Izaak used to eat them, whereas modern anglers put them back in the river. Those interested in such matters may be intrigued by the following recipe. It is not as elaborate as Walton's, which involves spit-roasting, verjuice, and equipment now found only in the casualty departments of our teaching hospitals. It was given to me by Gaston Grandbouffe, proprietor of the Auberge *Mon Repos* in the Gorge des Goules, an almost other-wordly eating place behind the Cimetière Marin at Villecrevée.

Take one medium-sized male chub. Place him on a large wooden board. Remove his scales, and cut with a razor large slits in his skin. Place in the slits medallions of garlic, truffle and oysters. Then baste the whole with any tart white wine – Gaston uses Château Nécropole, an astringent flinty *côte de nuits* – smear liberally with butter into which has been flogged a hint of asafetida, and throw it to the pigs. The board may be eaten if desired, since Gaston maintains stoutly that it tastes better than the chub. My own personal preference is for burning it, in a closed stove.

The wind abated slightly at about lunchtime, enabling me to pass under Moulsford railway bridge, catch a brief glimpse of the Downs, and flog on past Pangbourne and Sonning.

Even fifty-yard visibility cannot mar the attraction of Pang-bourne Reach. The north bank springs out of the river with commendable vigour, not tiring until it has reached an altitude of more than 200 feet, which in the Thames Valley is a tremendous height. The bank is thick with large and ancient oaks, beeches and chestnuts, and they glowed like a bonfire among the skeins of rain. The river itself was solemn, black and powerful. On it swam thousands of coots, invisible in the gloom but for the white patches on their foreheads, which bobbed along like midget ghosts tremendously agitated about something. Among the coots, like destroyers among bumboats, swam the grebes.

The grebe is one of the rare successes of species preservation. Victorian and Edwardian ladies felt that hats were incomplete without the feathers of at least one grebe, and milliners armed with twelve-bore shotguns did fearful execution. They were saved by the simultaneous invention of non-lethal birdwatching (a Victorian birdwatcher did not consider a bird properly watched until he could examine it daily in a nice glass case) and the decline in fashionableness of feathery hats. Then in 1914 Julian Huxley peeping-tommed their bizarre courtship dance and wrote about it skilfully and at length; whereupon the world realized that your average grebe was not merely a chunk of plumage ripe for the plucking or hollowing out, but a fascinating bird of huge personal integrity. As a result, there are stretches of the Thames on which an icebreaker or grebesweeper is more or less *de rigueur* if the oarsman is not to grind to a grebe-clogged halt.

At the bottom of the reach, Pangbourne College's boathouse had vomited forth the usual assortment of racing boats on to the river. We went through them in a moist and lacklustre manner; they were all pairs and fours, and the important thing with a pair or four is to keep out of its way. Then, by the quickening of *Magdalen*'s antique bones, I knew she had spotted a sculler. I turned, hand raised in salutation; I come (I prepared to say) bringing greetings from Powys and the earldoms of the Marches. Fleet brother in oarsmanship, hail from the wild lands! But as I opened my mouth to speak, the sculler looked over his shoulder. He had a beard, and cross-eyes. His lips moved first. 'Why don't you get out of the way in that f—ing bathtub,' he said, and shot past before I could brain him.

The rain continued to fall.

Willows wept inconsolably beside boathouses rotting from the ground up, roofs sagging like hammocks, carpenters' gingerbread eaves fuzzy with soaking moss. There was a sense that everything in the landscape was asleep and slumping slowly but inevitably into the river. Thoughts of the finite nature of human existence crowded thick and fast. Thoughts of the finite nature of my tolerance for this extreme form of masochism came thicker and faster. Having succeeded in orienting myself on the Ordnance Survey map, and being within view of a church clock (my alarm clock, like everything else, was by now full of water) I timed myself over the measured mile. It took me a couple of minutes over half an hour with a crosswind. There were fifty miles to Teddington Lock, where the tidal Thames begins.

Today was Wednesday. Spurred on by my epicurean fantasies, I had notified the support group that I would be arriving at Westminster at noon on Sunday, so I was in trouble.

I pressed on through the thickening rain, arriving in the dripping dusk at Mapledurham Lock.

Thames Conservancy lock-keepers go off duty at teatime. This does not mean that the locks are closed, simply that the traveller must open them alone. They are at this stage of the river very large and operated by hydraulics. What with one thing and another it takes half an hour to get through. As I was closing the gates, a jaunty cove in a Tyrolean hat loomed out of the now total darkness, and said I was late. I agreed and asked him if there was anywhere I could camp, downriver, that was. Oh, no, he said, nearest site's miles away. Well, perhaps they wouldn't notice in the grounds of Mapledurham House – I'll nip up and ask, I said. Oh, no, they don't like that, said the man. Glad I'm not in your boots, ho, ho. His chuckles receded into the night. As I climbed into *Magdalen* I could not help reflecting that there had been something terribly *Midlands* about him.

Outside the lock gates, the current caught me. The weir pool was a vague patch of whiteness, roaring. The rain lashed down; on the far bank, the chimneys and gables of Mapledurham House came and went in the twilight. *Magdalen* slewed away downstream. The banks shot past. I kept her in midstream as far as possible, head down to stop the rain trickling down my neck. My left oar touched something hard; there was a scraping under the keel and *Magdalen*'s stem slammed into something large and solid. Water piled under her port side, and she began to slew. I backed water, but she was stuck fast. The river roared under the hull as I heaved with an oar against a large, bulky object: an island.

An island?

On an island there might be a flat spot on which a tent might be pitched.

Ten minutes later I was grovelling up a forty-five degree slope with the mooring line between my teeth and mud like melted chocolate squashing between my fingers. I got the tent up by torchlight, sheltering periodically in a hollow tree. Then I lay awake all night while the rain thundered on the canvas. At times there was a harder edge to the thunder, as the trains roared along the high brick embankment that prefaces Reading.

They say that Galsworthy had Soames Forsyte die at Mapledurham. If I did not know better I would lay good odds he died of a mixture of despair and drowning.

It is definitely a mistake to wish for a strong current, if you are an air-breathing creature. Thanks to my expressed preference in the matter, it was still raining when dawn crept unwillingly down the hundred-foot gap between the river and the clouds. In the hurly-burly of the previous night the jam-jar had been left in the boat, so I drank my morning coffee out of the saucepan. The ground was as slippery as if it had been greased, and while I heaved the container and the other junk down the bank I fell several times, coating myself with liquid mud until I must have looked like a train crash in a chocolate factory. Then I climbed in, and the day began.

People had been shaking their heads for the past three weeks. But on this morning, they made a movement of the head like a hen spotting a viper, with a simultaneous hiss of indrawn breath. Many of them saw the towrope I held up in the air; many of them passed, oblivious to the cracked curses raining after them. But finally, as *Magdalen* drifted past the encroaching red brick of Reading, a giant hire boat slowed and took the rope. A mug of soup came over the stern. The raindrops made little craters in the stuff. The cook watched me. It was packet chunky beef in a tin mug. It seared the lips, and imparted a welcome glow. Handing back the mug, I watched four girls between the ages of eleven and fourteen giggle at me from the stern of the hire boat. One of them looked a bit like Pallas Athene, if you can imagine Pallas Athene based in Mitcham. They all agreed that I talked posh but did not look posh, which was the understatement of the year. Pallas Athene watched in horror as I breakfasted off cold tinned sausages, cold baked beans, Worcester sauce and cold rainwater. Then she spoke of her boyfriend. Why did she need a boyfriend, I asked. Because without one, she said (her eyes melting), she would be lonely. Her younger sister rolled her eyes heavenwards and began to speak, rapidly and with passion, of her Staffordshire bull terrier. It could chomp a full baked-bean tin in half with its molars, she said, which was more than Pallas Athene's boyfriend could do. I was about to observe that I betted the boyfriend had a tin opener, when we arrived at Sonning and slipped the tow.

As *Magdalen* came to the oars in midstream, a voice hailed us from the bank. 'Fancy a cup of soup?' Grinning weakly, I rowed ashore. It was about eleven o'clock. A thin woman with grey hair, an Aertex shirt and goosepimples handed me a mug of packet chicken noodle over the side of a semi-derelict wooden cabin cruiser. Then she disappeared below. The soup slid down, mingling uneasily with its predecessor. The woman reappeared. "Good soup,' I said, imagining that we would now discourse freely on mixed topics. 'Thank you.'

'Soup's hot,' she said. 'Hot and nice. Goodbye.'

And I was on my way.

Downstream there are huge flat islands covered with golden chestnut trees. Among the islands swim great rafts of mallard and grebe. The river was empty here, pocked with the rain. A red Queen Anne house stood back on a rise and surveyed its chestnuts with pride. Soon afterwards, the houses of the River Rich commenced; clapboard and thatch, brick and plate glass, eaves and dormers, mansards and turrets, dropped in the middle of vast green lawns unmarked by human foot. Most of them were empty.

It was lunchtime. That morning, the pouring of the rain had suggested soup instead of coffee in the thermos. Lunch consisted of cheese, biscuits, more beans and tinned sausages and more Worcester sauce with more rainwater. It seemed as if it might be a wise move to tip the soup into the river, but this notion produced screams of anguish from the 25% Scottish corpuscles strolling through my venous system. The soup was therefore drunk. After all, I told myself, it's highly unlikely that I'll be offered any more.

The first lock after lunch was Marsh Lock. It drew near in an empty river. Then suddenly the water was covered with giant noddy boats, all racing for the entrance in a fog of exhaust smoke and a crackle of fibreglass. Having insinuated *Magdalen* into a position where she was unlikely to get crushed, I took a look around. It was a bit like being a sardine canapé stranded among the cakes at a mass wedding. On all sides were glistening white hulls topped with radomes and tuna towers and fifteen-foot whip aerials. CB radios chattered in cabins with floral curtains drawn against the rain. Exhausts bubbled like old men's stomachs. The paddles opened, and half a million pounds dropped a yard or so. The gates commenced swinging back.

I looked up, catching the eye of a man in a denim cap (I assumed it was his eye: it was hard to be sure, because he was wearing dark glasses) and said in fluent Canalese, 'Gie's a snatch to the next lock, eh?'

He said, 'What?'

'A tow,' said I.

'Oh, a tow! Why didn't you say so in the first place?'

And there I was, hitched up, when his wife appeared from the lower regions. She was a small woman with a stern eye, and she was carrying a tray. On the tray were three mugs of soup. 'You'll have some,' she said, fixing me with the peeper.

'Oh. Yup. Super,' I said feebly, looking about me.

Though it sounds ungrateful, I nearly tipped that soup into my boot. The wheelhouse stretched away like a prairie on all sides. No cover. Also, I had removed my boots. There was nothing for it. I raised the cup to my lips. Deep in the system, Etna stirred. Keeping the lid firmly on it, I said, 'Excellent. Capital. Soup,' and drank.

For the record, it was cream of tomato (tinned).

We motored for two hours. Henley went past. At Temple Lock, the lady spoke disparagingly of lock-keepers who threw away or burned driftwood. Driftwood was vital for floral art. She went below. Her husband groped for the throttles, blind as a bat in his dark glasses, and spoke of the inadequacies of canal craft. He was having a lovely time. So was I: *Magdalen* bobbed merrily astern, and I was warm and dry. The saloon was done in chocolate brown, the galley in cocoa cork to deaden sound. As I peered forward and below, the lady emerged from the galley with a tray. On the tray were three mugs. 'Packet asparagus,' she chirped. 'Thought it'd make a nice change.'

They released me at Cookham, and I rowed down to the lock, sloshing internally. In the lock, a person with a moustache, dressed in oilskins from crown of head to toe of foot, was trying to tie up a narrow boat. He walked up to the gate gear (the lock-keeper, needless to say, was off duty) and began twiddling.

Turning the wheel at a lock does one of two things: it either operates the sluices or the gates. You tell the wheel which you want it to do by throwing a two-position switch, marked on one position GATES and the other SLUICES, to GATES if you want gates and SLUICES if you want sluices. Clear? The man with the moustaches, obviously an original thinker, had the switch at GATES and was experiencing some difficulty in turning the wheel, because he was fighting the weight of the top four feet of the Thames as far back as Lechlade. He looked as if he had been there for some time.

I said, 'You'd better do the switch.'

He said, screwing up his face, 'Wha'?'

I threw the switch. 'That thing.'

He beamed, the light of pure deafness suffusing his face. 'How do you do, Mr King,' he said. 'Watson's the name. On holiday from Hong Kong.'

'Ah,' I said. 'Kowloon and so on.'

He squinted at the sky. 'Not tonight. Too much cloud.'

This was all very baffling. It must be something to do with his hood, I suspected. I assisted him with the wheel. When we had finished I saluted his extremely pretty girlfriend. 'Gosh,' she said. 'You do look wet. Humphrey, do let's stop and give the poor man something.'

Humphrey obeyed with a poorish grace. It was nearly dark. Sun over yard-arm. My whisky was long gone. This would be the much-needed stiffener . . .

'Soup,' said the girlfriend. 'Label was off the tin, so I don't know what it is. Still, it'll warm you up.'

It tasted like bat seethed in camel's milk.

Three-quarters of an hour later I was camping in pitch blackness on another island. This one was in Cliveden Reach, about a foot above the river level. At long last, the river was rising.

In the morning, I lay dozing in the mulch of goose-down that had once been my sleeping bag, trying to put off the evil hour when I would have to crawl into the rain. Gradually, remorselessly, my eyelids separated. At first all I could see was the green firmament of the tent roof, frosted with glittering jewels of rain, and socks hanging from the ridge poles, dripping. I rolled over to turn on the weather forecast—

In the corner of the tent a dwarf was standing watching me. At my shout of horror, mallards' wings whirred outside. I plunged from the bed, scattering stove and saucepans and food buckets. The dwarf pitched forwards on to his face. I knew there was something wrong with him; he did not have a face to fall on to. He was my Barbour jacket, stiff with wet. I lay back weakly, heart hammering. Then I stood it up again and put the stove inside it while I eased out of my sleeping bags and into a few jerseys. Steam was issuing from the neckhole and sleeves of the jacket by now; putting it on was a bit like climbing into a Turkish bath. On the radio, a weather person probably wearing a light nylon shirt and summerweight Dacron slacks was saying that he was afraid the weather picture was not a pretty one, because the low with associated troughs had caught its kilt on a barbed-wire fence and was now sulking somewhere near Aberdeen. I switched him off. A noise that had been lurking in the background of consciousness now leaped to the centre of the stage. It was the rushing of mighty waters, and it seemed remarkably close.

It was.

Last night the river had been a good twenty feet away. Today it had come about fifteen feet closer, and only the fact that I had accidentally pitched the tent on a slight elevation had prevented the Thames from flowing straight through it and me.

There followed a few moments' sweating. Just downstream was Boulter's Weir. Another couple of yards to the right and I would have been . . . well, horribly mangled. As it was, there were problems, the most serious of which was that *Magdalen* was tied to a tree in what was now a thriving torrent of ugly brown water. Raising the hem of my garments, I tiptoed down to her. The water was cold. The mud was slippery, and full of roots. By the time I had dragged her back to the tent I had fallen over once, and any wetness I had experienced on waking seemed but a passing breath of moisture.

The landscape had changed completely. Yesterday, Cliveden Reach had been a stately procession of water rolling past steep woods. Today it was a flume of swirling cocoa, from which stunted trees projected, bent over by the piling waters. The sky was no longer an oppressive grey blanket; above the hills, it was ragged with piles of black cloud and streaks of white, and even, here and there, a shred of blue. It all looked very dangerous; a gunfighting sort of day, that would tear you up as soon as look at you. It was also strangely exhilarating.

Magdalen was leaking again. I pumped her out in a cursory manner; I wanted to be away. Loading the gear, I climbed in and let go the mooring rope. The current caught hold and whirled us like a dead leaf across what yesterday had been dry land. We sidled into the main stream; the bank flashed by, and suddenly the danger posts for Boulters Weir were coming up and we were struggling out of the stream and into the lock cut. The lock-keeper had just finished checking his rain gauge. He looked depressed, but when he saw us he seemed to cheer up. It was as if he had seen something extremely amusing. I asked him how much it had rained in the night. He said an inch and a half.

Below Boulters, there are more islands, directly in the path of the weir stream. The river was running even faster here; hire boats were shooting about the river like pigs on an ice rink. One of them attempted to change lanes in the face of an oncoming island, missing it by inches.

At such times, the navigator feels as if he is caught in a film, of which he is not the director. Everything is moving except him, and his usual aids – propeller, rudder, distress signals – are entirely useless, as in one of those nightmares in which you are fleeing from bears across lakes of treacle. The propellers roar, the wheel is held hard over. The island comes inexorably on. The confident bite their fingernails down to the knuckle. The less confident prepare to abandon ship. The foresighted try to work out whether or not it is too late to stop the deposit cheque they have given the hire company.

There was a look of some smugness on the face of the fellow who had just missed the island. Magellan probably looked the same, after discovering the Straits. I was now, thanks to the current, travelling at the same speed as him, so I was able to observe his movements during the next ten minutes, something for which I shall be everlastingly grateful.

His boat was called something like the *Scarlet Woman*. Thames hirers all call their boats something like that, and there is a large fleet of *Women* of one kind and another. He was obviously intending to return his boat to base, which was a large gaggle of *Women* tied up half a mile below the islands. To this end his female companion went and stood at the bow, holding the mooring line in a state of readiness and casting the occasional horrified glance at the chicken houses and oak trees hurtling past on the current. The skipper lit a cigarette and clipped it jauntily between his lips. He approached the quay unconventionally, going downstream. Ten seconds before impact, he realized that this was not the right thing to do, since his engines had been full astern for half a minute and he was still travelling at ten miles an hour. He therefore put his rudder over. The tail whipped round like a rattlesnake, striking the concrete wall sharply. He staggered, and his companion, who had ceased to scream and was now busy gaping, would have gone overboard if she had not fallen into the rail. During the stagger, he had knocked the boat out of gear. Now he engaged forward, slammed his wheel over to port and swallowed his cigarette. Twenty yards downstream, the *Women* were moored five abreast. The *Scarlet Woman* turned until her longitudinal axis was at right angles to the quay, and her entire side was presented to the current. The female companion was climbing to her feet looking astern and offering noisy advice to the skipper, who was doubled over his belly, coughing and moaning by turns. Stung by her insults, he straightened up and offered a spirited defence. In the heat of the argument neither of them saw that they were travelling sideways, under the razor-sharp bows of the moored *Women*. Until, that is, it was too late.

The last I saw of them, the companion had scrambled on to a moored *Woman* and was still shouting. The captain, who must have heard that you go down with your ship, was heading into the cabin. Rending noises were becoming audible above the screaming. And somewhere in Maidenhead, the fleet operator was cashing the deposit cheque.

The next lock is Bray. Here the weir, instead of being tucked safely away behind an island, runs where the right-hand bank of the lock cut ought to be. Under normal circumstances it is possible to slink down the left-hand bank untroubled by the weir stream. With the river up and roaring, the weir stream extends all the way to the left bank, leaving no room for rowing boats. (Marlow is even worse, but I had passed it under tow and also under the influence of soup, and had therefore not noticed it.)

I sloped along the left bank, but row as I would, the stream had me. It runs straight towards the lock cut, then, dammed by the still water in front of the gates, turns sharp right. The idea was to ride the current until the last minute, then give a powerful twitch of the left oar that would pluck *Magdalen* out of it and into the still water. It was not quite as easy as that: once the current had got

Magdalen's keel in its teeth, it did not want to let go. I pulled once with the left oar; no result. And again; again no result, and by this time we were in the crook of the stream, and the lock cut had opened before my eyes and was closing again. One more pull put her beam-on, and then I rowed both together, sixty strokes to the minute, for two minutes, and we were into the eddy at the mouth of the cut, spinning; and then on down, with the distant figure of the lock-keeper leaning on his gates, looking worried but tactful.

It was here that I noticed that the boards were up.

The boards are attached to the lock gates in times of flood. They bear dire warnings about the next weir downstream. The fact that they are being displayed means that all hire craft must tie up pending the arrival of licensed pilots, who will drive them back to base.

The tussle with the weir stream had left the heart thudding and the brow bedewed. As I rowed down the cut towards the lock, however, the amazing self-healing powers of the human imagination had gone to work. It was probably just a bad weir, I told myself. It's been raining; of course there's a trickle of water in the river. Anyway, you were praying for rain only yesterday. Well, you got it, you use it.

But the red boards changed everything. If the current was reckoned by those who knew to be too much for motor boats, where did it leave lone oarsmen in leaking hulks? Nowhere, was where. And probably . . . horribly mangled.

Matters were getting serious.

At ten o'clock the clouds parted and the sun streamed down. It lit a scene of awful devastation.

The river had become a mud-coloured torrent that hurled itself down straight reaches, and when it came to corners rushed round the outside of the bend, ignoring the inside, which therefore became an eddy studded with holes. These holes were not large, but they made a sound like a blue whale sucking its teeth. On this waste of water there slid a variety of hire cruisers with fluorescent orange notices in their windows, signifying that there was a pilot on board. The approaches to Boveney Lock resembled the final stages of a Space Invaders game. One of the cruisers slid across my bows. A window opened and a Palestinian terrorist wearing a pilot's badge stuck his head out. 'Where's Sunbury?' he asked in a thick Lebanese accent. Behind him, his hostages huddled white-faced, passing a half-bottle of gin from hand to hand.

The weir at Boveney is more conveniently placed than the one at Bray. A raft of mallard were, however, in the process of being swept over as we entered the gates. The notice said the lock-keeper was on the weir. After ten minutes he came back. You could see by the look in his spectacles that there was trouble in store.

This lock-keeper has the seen-it-all, totally competent expression of a very experienced policeman, probably the result of many summers spent watching Eton boys trying to drown themselves in his front garden. He walked to the side of the lock and gazed thoughtfully down at *Magdalen*. He said: 'I've just been on the weir. I was pulling out the last of the paddles. Do you know what that means?'

'Lot of water,' I said weakly. 'Been raining.'

'The river,' he said, as if to an idiot child, 'is in full flood. You should seriously consider getting out of it, because the next weir is no good.'

'Oh, we'll be all right,' I said. 'Come all the way from Wales, you know.'

The spectacles remained on us. Then he shrugged his shoulders and walked away.

The word 'serious' seemed to be cropping up rather a lot at the moment.

From the parapet of Windsor Bridge, Romney Weir was a line of dirty foam. Downstream of the bridge piers the eddies were bona fide whirlpools, their holes big enough to drop a dustbin down without its touching the sides. Tracing the main current with my eye, I saw that the back-eddies after the arches all ended in the weir stream; there was absolutely no chance of getting into the lock cut. It was an absolute certainty that both I and *Magdalen* would be horribly mangled. I watched the river for half an hour, trying to work out a way. There was none. But what were the alternatives?

The alternative was to get the boat out of the water, organize a trailer and go home. After nineteen days on the water, bleeding, blue and sodden, we were finished.

It was all over.

I returned to *Magdalen* to break the news and find somewhere she could be got at with a trailer.

Just above Eton College rafts was moored a distinguished narrow boat in rifle-brigade green. Painted on her cabin was the name *Dyfed*.

'Hello,' said Bingo Smail. 'You again? We're off to London in half an hour. Fancy a tow?'

CHAPTER ELEVEN

Windsor to Westminster

I hand over to fifty horses – A gnome's graveyard in Staines – Terrors of the tideway – Cogitations on the tide – The joys of Little Venice – A tumult on the river – A noddy boat to the rescue – The debate continues – I grow up – I act irresponsible – Westminster or bust – Westminster

The view from a narrow boat's tiller is a heartening one. You feel high in the air, able to see for miles. The hull bites the water hard, responding instantly to tiny adjustments of the rudder. The engine thunders under your feet. And astern, *Magdalen* rides high in the water, always gliding down the first wave of the wash.

Old Windsor Lock was behind us, as was Windsor Bridge. The eddies were bad; a couple of times, Bingo had had to put the throttle on to its slops to power out of a whirlpool. But those fifty horses had done it; you could imagine them, large and chestnut-coloured with shaggy white fetlocks, steaming in the sun on the towpath. Bingo and I stood leaning on the cabin top and watched the world go by, and spoke of one thing and another, and London came to meet us at a steady eight knots. Houses thickened down to the river; in the middle of the afternoon we moored at Staines.

On the right bank of the river in Staines there is a bit of garden sculpture worth a pilgrimage. Three life-sized fibreglass mermaids sit on a rockery, staring at the river. They are combing their long hair and pouting. They have enormous bosoms with pert pink nipples, and they are sucking in their stomachs and turning coyly away from the prurient gaze of noddy-boat folk. They have huge scaly hips, swelling from tiny waists: 42 – 23 – 60p a pound. The riverbed in front of their jetty is probably littered with garden gnomes who have died for love.

That night I slept in *Dyfed's* saloon. It was a curious feeling, being warm enough and dry enough and nearly at the end of the line. After the Smails had gone to their cabin, I went out on to the stern. *Magdalen* was swinging a little at her tow. She looked very small behind the narrow boat, loaded down with equipment as

[183]

she was. She had a sort of forgotten look not unlike the one she had had when I had first seen her at Ringstead Bay. 'All right, old thing?' I said.

She stirred on the towline, the current making a bow wave that shone brave silver in the moonlight. She was all right.

Downstream Penton Hook Weir roared, and the lights of London threw their dirty reflection at the sky.

Tomorrow, the tideway.

Next morning we passed through Penton Hook Lock, noting the large lumps out of the concrete banks where hire boats had overcompensated after extracting themselves from the weir stream, and continued downstream. The river here winds through a maze of reservoirs and embankments, before arriving at Weybridge. After Weybridge the scene becomes brisk and bustling with squads of little kayak artistes following their instructors like ducklings pursuing mallards, and outrageous houseboat conversions with pigeons roosting in their pocky hulls and no visible bow or stern. The most adventurous of these was a small caravan welded into a large rubbish skip.

According to those who navigate the non-tidal Thames, taking a rowing boat on the tideway is a better way of killing yourself than putting a loaded shotgun in your mouth and pulling the trigger. There is a chatty little leaflet, issued at locks, called the *Tideway Guide*, which is full of baffling information about tides and horn signals and wisps of straw displayed in the arches of bridges to signify restricted headroom. Its overall effect is as threatening as a ransom note; can one, the oarsman asks himself, digest all this information and row at the same time? *Magdalen*, bobbing along astern, was looking excessively small.

What started as a small germ of unease very soon became abject terror. Thanks to the rain there was an uprecedented quantity of water rushing out to sea. It was the wettest October since records began; most of the wetness had fallen in the Thames Valley, and it is a matter of history that the day on which *Magdalen* was to brave the tideway was scheduled as being the day of heaviest run-off.

Bingo Smail was more of a freshwater man than a tideway man. He advised me strongly to take to the canals with him; he would tow me down to Brentford, and then I could go through the locks with him and up the Hanworth flight and end the journey in Little Venice. I looked at maps and gnawed my fingernails, experiencing the same humiliating series of emotions as when faced with the Wast Hill tunnel. We passed through Teddington Lock, where lock-keepers in white caps eyed *Magdalen* and shook their heads. Kayak fiends were sporting in the weir. The river itself looked as if it was suffering from a serious eruptive rash: there were holes in it, and humps and writhing creases and boils, constantly changing places with each other until it looked as if Father Thames was not so much flowing as chewing his way towards the sea. I heard a heavily life-jacketed kayaker say to a friend on the bank that he was getting out of this because it was too ruddy dangerous. The canals were the only *sensible* way.

Come on, yellow-belly, I said. You won't capsize *Magdalen*. Not in a hundred years. Floats like a cork (here the eyes strayed to the six inches of black, oily water that had accumulated in her bilges during the past hour).

We had been waiting below the lock. Now we set off downstream. Bingo wanted to go and see a friend (Wonderful chap. Ghastly varicose veins, knows everything there is to know about the coffee bean) and attempted to put *Dyfed* head to stream. He slammed the tiller over. The landscape began to revolve. Slowly, the nose came across the stream, until the long axis of the boat was at right angles to the bank. It took five minutes of roaring and juddering for the stern to come round and after that, we inched upstream, full throttle at a quarter of a knot. This, mark you, was fifty horsepower. The friend was out.

I was scheduled to arrive at noon the following day, at Westminster Pier. Provided I could stay the right way up, getting there was no problem. The tide was low at noon, and I would have the last of the ebb, allied with a chronic flood, under the keel. The sound barrier would be quivering on the tip of *Magdalen*'s nose.

What worried me was how to *stop*.

If the river flowed at five knots, and my maximum in still water was two knots, any attempt at rowing upstream would leave me travelling backwards at a brisk jog. And if I missed Westminster Pier, it was next stop Holland.

So I decided to take the canals, and sat cursing myself as we roared down the turbulent river under a piercing blue sky. On the margins of Syon Park, herons appeared completely unworried by the fact that they were a mere 50p tube ride from Piccadilly Circus. Locks. Filthy water. I had no desire to go on the canals. Lovely as Little Venice might be . . .

The rain had been falling all morning. The canal ran under the Westway for much of its length; the man in the dirty white boat was deaf in both ears. He had passed Wormwood Scrubs Prison and Kensal Green Cemetery, admiring the little trap-doors where the bodies were popped through the wall from the funeral barges. The sides of the canal were black with soot. Humanoids with shaven heads and enormous boots lumbered on the far side of the high wire fences enclosing the ribbon of black water, and threw empty bottles and bricks.

He rowed on.

After seven hours' unremitting toil, the bottom boards were awash with blood from his ruined hands. He turned his head for what must have been the millionth time; his oarstrokes quickened, as if with hope. For what is this? Ahead, houses are painted white. Green trees grow. A sign creaks in the wind: The Public House of Destination.

The rower's back straightens. The stern of the white boat ploughs a proud furrow in the black waters, ready for the shower of rose-petals and champagne corks, the cheers of the well-wishers, the sight of the certain face above all other faces . . .

The white boat comes alongside. The quay is empty, but for horizontal rain. The rower splashes across to the door marked 'Saloon'. 'Sorry' says the landlord. 'We're closed. Are you the bloke was rowing?'

Modestly, the man assents.

"There's a 'alf of shandy under the flowerpot,' says the man.

'*They all went an hour ago. Mind you bring back the glass.*'

This was by no means satisfactory. But would the river be any better?

The cheering started at Hammersmith Bridge. It was almost loud enough to drown the band playing Handel's Water Music *on the poop of the* Mary Rose, *specially refurbished for the occasion. On the banks the crowds began running, jostling good-humouredly round the fountains filled with Bollinger by the GLC. In the centre of the river, the man in the impeccable white suit with the Panama hat and twelve-inch cigar waved negligently, and rowed on. Clouds of white doves erupted from moored lighters. The cheering was a constant dull roar now; chunks of sound-loosened masonry fell from Lambeth Bridge, and on the terrace of the House of Commons Mark Heathcote Amory and Dennis Skinner embraced gleefully as the cheering found form: HE MADE IT, chanted nine million throats. HE MADE IT! The face of Big Ben cracked, riven by the cheering; the clock stopped, and it was unanimously decided that it would be left at that time in perpetuity, as a reminder. And a beautiful woman in a flowing Schiaparelli dress waited on Westminster Pier, a little curly-haired boy holding either hand.*

'*Why are they cheering?*' *said the larger of the boys.*

'*They are cheering for your Daddy,*' *said the woman.* '*For he has made it.*'

'Fancy a cheese sandwich?' said Dilys Smail.

We had passed the London Apprentice. The floodtide was on the river now; the willows swam like mangroves on the metal shield of the water. A coffee-and-cream cabin cruiser was performing mysterious evolutions, as if searching for a U-boat with its sonar equipment. Bingo frowned, shifting his grip on the tiller. 'What the hell that bloody noddy boat is doing we shall never know,' he said.

For the first time in our aquaintance he was wrong.

The captain of the noddy boat cupped his hands around his mouth. 'Have you got someone called Sam on board?' he shouted. 'Because I've just met his wife at the London Apprentice, and she wants to know if he fancies a drink.'

★

I would not need all the gear the following day, so we unloaded it at the slipway in front of the London Apprentice. Out it all came: the water canister, still reeking of Coca-Cola, the basket, now containing only the few tins of fish paste I had been unable to face; the yellow box, covered in greenish algae; the container, sloshing as it rolled up the slip; the tent and the camp-bed, landing on the tarmac in a spreading pool of their own water; the food boxes and toolkit and guitar and fishing rod, the paddle and pole, spare rope and tarpaulin; all the clutter and junk I had hauled for three hundred miles, up to and including the porridge and muesli that had burst its bags and mingled with the filth in the bilges to form a jelly-like slime three inches deep. Already it seemed like the debris of another life; and *Magdalen* was a little less *Magdalen* and a little more just an old boat well into its dotage.

It was an evening far removed from Camping Gaz stoves and wet sleeping bags. It was strange to be under a roof again, and in a fish restaurant, drinking Pouilly-Fumé instead of mild ale, and talking to people I had met before, and would meet again. It was strange to be lying in a huge soft bed that smelt of flowers.

The bed was too soft. Sleep would not come.

I had done the sensible thing and decided to take to the canals. I had telephoned the Thames Conservancy and they said straight out that only suicidal maniacs would be on the river the next day. It was a decision taken after mature reflection and with an adult wisdom I was surprised to discover in myself. It certainly bore no resemblance to the spirit in which I had commenced this undertaking. I turned the pillow over, looking for the cool side. Amazing how one's judgement matures in twenty-one short days, I thought, folding my hands smugly on the breast and composing my mind.

LILY-LIVERED SPINELESS PUSILLANIMOUS CHICKEN-HEARTED HERRING-GUTTED SCUM, roared the conscience. REMEMBER THE BURE DISASTER. NEVER MIND DEATH, IF YOU DON'T GET TO PARLIAMENT YOU DON'T DESERVE TO LIVE.

'Oh, all right,' I groaned. Then, surprisingly, I went to sleep.

Next morning I rang the river police and explained what I intended to do, which was to arrive alongside Westminster Pier at noon. Could they, I inquired, act as wicket-keeper?

The voice on the other end was surprisingly cheerful for 6 a.m. It said it would look forward to it. It also said that there was no problem and anyway they were testing the Woolwich flood barrier, which ought to smooth things out a little. I told Karen about the flood barrier. It seemed to ease her mind. It certainly eased mine.

So in I piled.

The river was going like a train under a thick coating of fog. It was grey and mysterious, but smooth as cream, and flowing four knots.

By Hammersmith Bridge the sun was up; by Putney it was throwing the shadows of riverside buildings huge in the fog and transforming into giants by Sickert the men wading for dace. The mist lifted: Fulham Palace suddenly blazed with sunlight. After three weeks of ploughing fresh water with her ancient belly, *Magdalen* felt the salt even through the filth of the tideway. She swooped in the flume under Albert Bridge and skittered like a salmon in an eddy below Cadogan Pier.

I was running half an hour early, so just below Vauxhall Bridge I tucked her into the eddy behind one of the piers, and she sat good as gold, while I watched the seagulls fighting the rats for offal in front of the sculpture by Henry Moore. As we sat I repented of the way we had grown apart, and told her in a sentimental undertone that she had been very good and kind; forgetting, as was only polite, the wallows and wambles and those soaking interviews under sheets of polythene where the air was unbreathable with the stink of plastic padding and silicone caulker. And she replied in her turn that it had all been very interesting, and that she hoped when I had given her back to her proprietor I could come and paint her again, one day. I told her it was not over yet; there was Westminster Pier to come alongside. Deep in the seat that bore my weight I seemed to hear woody, patronizing laughter.

Then under the red spans of Lambeth Bridge a river police launch showed, a grey moustache under her bow. She came alongside. For the last time I pushed the hands forward, dug in the blades, and shifted that seven hundred pounds of soggy mahogany into the current.

The breeze stirred the Red Ensign at her transom as the Houses of Parliament came up black and gold on the port bow. She dug in her keel and ran like an arrow under the shrill wailing of the reception committee on Westminster Bridge, and came alongside the pier so neatly that I did not even notice what had happened until it was done. Champagne corks whizzed about a bit. We pulled her out, and I stood in the crowd of Japanese tourists piling on to the sightseeing steamers and remembered standing under the huge green dome of Plynlimmon, looking down the Severn valley and wondering if it was possible. It seemed that it was. Somebody asked what all the fuss was about. I told him that I had just rowed from Wales. He asked me why.

This was a question I had asked myself standing next to the canoe as the chilly Severn flowed under Llanidloes Bridge. I had hoped to find out on the way. But had I? Certainly, I could now contemplate the Bure disaster with perfect equanimity. Certainly I had travelled under muscle power in regions where few had travelled this century, except with engines. And of course I had proved that the hitherto unused water route from Plynlimmon to the Houses of Parliament was feasible, which might be very useful to someone. Possibly they would wish to take a sheep to their MP, taking three weeks to do so. Though of course it was unlikely that the sheep would have survived. Marco Polo would not have recognized it as a valuable trade route on such grounds. No. None of these.

What about the Outward Bound factor, then? Had I learned new powers of leadership and self-reliance, out there in the rain? Certainly not. There had been no-one to lead, for one thing. For another, I had accepted far too many tows to justify the self-reliance claim. Well, had it been a pleasant holiday? Yes. It had. Season of mists and mellow fruitfulness; the acorns plopping into the Oxford Canal, the fiery walls of Pangbourne Reach, the goose-darkened sky of the Severn Valley. On the other hand, there had been the white zone of the Stratford on Avon; Leamington Spa; Reading; and a good deal of rain . . . a reasonable holiday. Fairly hard work, actually.

Well, what about the boat? Was it the challenge of rowing three hundred miles in a relic of the Age of Sail? I looked at *Magdalen*, remembering wallows to port, sideways wambles, and long, steady leaking. She was just a ghastly old tub, fit only to be filled with earth and used for the growing of polyanthuses. I felt a twinge of guilt at this disloyalty, but returned to the question. Why? There was no good reason. Except one, the usual one.

'Because,' I said, 'it was there.'

'Oh, ah.' He was wearing a brown coat of the kind popularized by grocers, and fiddling with his loose change. His eyes alighted on *Magdalen*. 'In *that*?' he said.

The vision of *Magdalen* planted with polyanthuses faded. In its place came the picture of a valiant blue-and-white craft piled with gear, plunging through the white horses of the dreaded Eymore Rapids; toiling hour after hour across the sunlit summit level of the Oxford Canal; of the same craft, stained with travel, bobbing like a cork on the bloated Thames above Windsor. Guilt surged over me. A lump, I tell you, rose in my throat.

'Her name,' I said, 'is *Magdalen*. And take your hands out of your pockets when you are speaking to a lady.'